PIANO BY HEART

MEMORIZE AND PERFORM YOUR MUSIC IN LESS TIME WITH FEWER TEARS

by
BERNARD M. PATTEN

PIANO BY HEART

MEMORIZE AND PERFORM YOUR MUSIC
IN LESS TIME WITH FEWER TEARS

Copyright © 2024 Bernard Michael Patten, M.D.

All rights reserved. No part of this publication may be reproduced, distributed, or transmitted in any form or by any means, including photocopying, recording, or other electronic or mechanical methods, without the prior written permission of the publisher, except in the case of brief quotations embodied in critical reviews and certain other noncommercial uses permitted by copyright law. Any perceived slight against any individual is purely unintentional.

For permission requests, write to the publisher at:
contact@identitypublications.com.

Ordering Information:
Quantity sales. Special discounts are available on quantity purchases by corporations, associations, and others. For details, contact the publisher at the address above.

Orders by U.S. trade bookstores and wholesalers.
Please contact Identity Publications:
Tel: (805) 259-3724 or visit www.IdentityPublications.com.

ISBN-13: 978-1-945884-88-7 (paperback)
ISBN-13: 978-1-945884-89-4 (hardcover)

First Edition
Publishing by Identity Publications.
www.IdentityPublications.com

Cover by Naira Aghayan

AB, Summa cum Laude, Columbia College
MD, College of Physicians and Surgeons, Columbia University
Fellow of the America College of Physicians
Fellow of the Royal Society of Medicine
Fellow of the Texas Neurological Society
Fellow of the American Academy of Neurology
Memory Fellow of the New York Academy of Medicine
Diplomate of the American Board of Psychiatry and Neurology
Formerly Instructor in Neuroscience, Philosophy and Mental Gymnastics at Rice University, School of Continuing Studies, Houston, TX

To St. Lidwina, patron saint of suffering

CONTENTS

Overture 1
Opus 1, No. 1 3
Chords as a Chunking Tool. 14
What This Book Does Not Cover 29
What Happens (Sometimes) When Composers Play Their Own
    Pieces—A Review of What Jimmy White Taught. 46
Introduction to the Science of Learning 60
Hermann Ebbinghaus' Experiments 62
The Cause of Most Memory Failures 71
Explicit Memory and Implicit Memory 93
Part II: Materials and Methods 107
How to Handle Mistakes. 124
Knowing Structure Is Important 137
Fracture Setting. 155

"The greater the ignorance the greater the dogmatism."
— Sir William Osler, M.D.

"The piano is a lovely instrument. You must fall in love with it, with its sound, and then be tender with it to make it, in turn, be sweeter to you. Herein"—and he laid his hand on the piano—"lies the divine beauty."
— Anton Rubinstein, in the fullness of his years and wisdom, quoted by Charles Cooke in *Playing the Piano for Pleasure*, 1941.

"If you have the notes to help you, then this stage-fright will take another form. Your touch gets uncertain; your rhythm is upset, and your tempo becomes hurried. Even if printed notes prevent a break-down, it is evident that they cannot prevent the worst fault of all—unmusical playing, which, rather than performance from memory, may be described as "playing without the music."
— Lilias Mackinnon, (*Music by Heart*, 1938) quoting and paraphrasing Ferruccio Busoni, *Von der Einheit der Musik*, 1922, Max Hesses Verlag, Berlin.

"Only two things provided refuge from the misery of life: music and cats."
— Albert Einstein

"All complain of want of memory, but none complain of want of judgment."
— Doctor Thomas Fuller (*Gnomologia*, 1732)

OVERTURE

◆ ◆ ◆

Greetings and welcome. This book is designed to encourage amateur piano players. It addresses three groups of amateurs:

1. Kids forced to play the piano by their parents.
2. Kids who enjoy playing the piano. There are such kids—I know because, in my youth, I was one of them.
3. Adults of three types:
Adults who played piano in their youth, gave it up, and now want to go back.
Adults who currently play the piano as a hobby and want to improve.
Adults who never played but want to play the piano as a hobby for entertainment and fun.

There are hundreds of thousands of you out there who, like me, love music and, like me, want to play better for the rest of our lives. Why the piano? Because it is a noble, self-sufficient instrument, almost a whole orchestra in and of itself, and it is the most popular musical instrument worldwide. There are literally hundreds of thousands of pianos in homes, studios, practice rooms at schools, and in nightclubs and restaurants. There are more pianos in existence than any other single musical instrument.

Furthermore, there are distinct advantages to being an amateur piano player. As an amateur, you get the fun of playing and, at the same time, you are free to do as you please. You are not constrained by the need to earn a living. The professional player often has to meet a schedule, play even when they don't feel like it, and travel to different venues to entertain paying and demanding audiences. Professionals often have to practice many hours a day, whereas you, as an amateur, need only practice as you please and see fit.

Three cheers for amateur playing! And cheers for amateur achievement!

In my opinion, music is a great force for developing breadth of character. Far too many students seem to be studying with a view to becoming a virtuoso. Forget that. The chance of that happening is close to zero. Since when did professional proficiency become a prerequisite for making music? Most of us cook but don't expect to win any Michelin stars. But if you want to be a virtuoso, that's good too.

Music, instead, should be studied and perfected for itself. Repeat: music should be studied and perfected for itself. The intellectual drill and thrills alone are of great value. Furthermore, (I learned this in my 80s) the study of music results in almost limitless gratification in old age because it lets you personally bring long-silent but beautiful scores to life on your own piano, in your own home, in your own time, at your own leisure, and in your own style and pace. And here is the free bonus: Our intelligence is malleable, not fixed, and can increase or decrease depending on how we use our brains. Mountains of evidence prove playing the piano increases brain power by actually forging new circuitry.

But why this book? Why did Doctor Patten write it?

Answer: Nowhere else is there a book that uses the scientific principles of human memory to help you memorize and play from memory the music you wish. In the history of piano instruction, this unique book is the first, best, worst, and only book that teaches you how to understand and use the basic principles of the neuroscience of memory to save you precious time and some tears. Music has been around probably for as long as humans have been around, but neuroscience, especially the neuroscience of memory, is recent. There are many personal stories of how people have memorized their music and many books that approach the subject. These anecdotal accounts can be moving and sometimes compelling. But as compelling as they may be, they cannot substitute for rigorous scientific research. As a scientist, I know ideas need to be tested by a variety of scientific methods to establish cause and effect, usefulness, efficacy, effectiveness, and ease of implementation. Medicine and science have a vast and exciting future. With this book, I aim to get my human touch and my human experience on the blueprints of the present state of the art of memory before AI takes over.

Prelude

There are as many schools of piano pedagogy as there are religions. And like religions, each seems to think it alone is in possession of the (divine?) truth. Let's face it: Most teachers will find something wrong with something I say in this book, and they may be right or they may be wrong. Be careful about what and with whom you study. Truth, in my view, is relative. What is true is true only for a particular time, place, situation, and person. Therefore, watch out! Don't over-exercise the believing sections of your mind. Take everything you are told as truth with a proverbial grain of salt. And yes, that includes what I say herein.

This is a personal book.

Here you have in your hand a personal book, full of personal observations, personal tidbits, and doodads (for I am a doodad person) that does not advocate dogma in any manner, shape, or form. I will always tell you what I think might be right and best, and I will try to mention other points of view. You have to decide what applies to you and your hobby of playing the piano, and you have to decide what doesn't apply to you and your hobby of playing the piano. After you have made these important decisions, act accordingly.

Summary of advice: Avoid dogma. Think for yourself.

OPUS 1, NO. 1

◆ ◆ ◆

Humbly do I present this book. As a child may sometimes see the significance of things unnoticed by an adult, as illustrated by the story of the Emperor's new clothes, so have I in my personal experience as a music student put my finger on some things the importance of which I feel has been hitherto somewhat neglected. The saving of time, the prevention of mental fatigue, the development of reliable memory, the fun and joy of performance, the promotion of self-esteem and confidence—how important are these to us amateur (and professional) pianists who want to have fun playing the piano, but don't want to make it a big deal or, for that matter, an ordeal or a torture.

The point about fun should not be taken lightly. The more fun you have doing something, the more you will want to do it. And the more you do it, the better you will get at it. Conclusion: FUN = GOOD.

Think of this: How rarely are these aforementioned desired items (like fun) considered by some teachers of music, where much of practice is "trial" and much of its results are "error." At times, the professional piano artist is not the best teacher, because, finding things out for herself/himself, she/he may leave the pupils to do likewise, with the result that many of the most useful ideas remain undeveloped for others, undeveloped in the dark room of the teacher's mind. If, as has been proven by experiment, both time and energy may be saved by a learner of nonsense syllables, as has been scientifically demonstrated many times by psychologists using special memory tricks (which I shall soon reveal), then surely something can be done to help a student learn and memorize something emotionally and intellectually stimulating and meaningful as a Beethoven sonata and still, in the process, have fun doing it.

My intention in this book, as an amateur who addresses amateurs, is inspirational, mainly to encourage children and adults whose hobby is playing the piano, or for that matter, any keyboard instrument. Based on my experiences at the piano as a student and my knowledge of the neurology of human memory, the book, written lightly, discursively, and I hope humorously, is intended to help you build a repertoire that can be played for fun from memory. Soon the music will be part of you and you will soon find much here to love.

Counterpoint

Want to be the life of the party? Here you will find concrete suggestions and many ideas, most of which can be understood and used by almost anyone. Repetition is the very soul and foundation of memory, so you will find lots of repetition in this book. Yes, there will be repetition time and time again. The repetitions are here to make sure the basic ideas get across and get into your memory and musical soul. Embrace repetition. It is your friend and will help you get more pleasure out of your hobby of playing the piano. You will learn more if you are happy at practice and consider it a fun thing to do and not a burden. The health value of making music can't be denied and should not be neglected. We humans are now in a mental health crisis with addiction, anxiety, and depression reaching epidemic proportions. Your music and your making it will evoke bliss, heart-filling satiation, and the remarkable gift of being mentally present in the zone.

Orchestration

To try to make this book useful to almost anyone, I hired music students, mainly boys and girls, to read this book and prescreen it for clarity. I paid them for their help and suggestions. Yes, in fact, eleven eager ten-to-seventeen-year-olds have read and worked on the text, and many have improved it with suggestions. Nice work, kids! Thanks a million.

Also, to improve the book in general, I am honored to have been helped by my music teachers. Madge Hunt read the manuscript, and so did Jimmy White. No two teachers are alike. Each has pluses and minuses. Madge did not think much of this book and said that I didn't know enough about music to write about it. On the other hand, Jimmy praised the work and made many excellent suggestions. I am also grateful to Ying Zhang for her excellent teaching, help, and suggestions. Amazingly, none of these three teachers entirely agree with each other on some issues. That is an important point to keep in mind because it means there is probably no absolutely correct approach to piano playing that applies to everyone. So, we must remain flexible and decide as individuals what works for us and what doesn't.

The point: Highly qualified teachers may have very different opinions. And such is life. Therefore, select your teacher to suit your own needs. Such needs will vary from time to time as you develop, learn more, or change your goals. Later we'll talk about how to select a teacher and how to deselect a teacher. By the way, if you think you can become a good pianist without a teacher, think again.

Ensemble

To illustrate the variety of teachers, I wish to tell you about my experiences.

Teacher One: Anna Platz taught me where middle C hangs out on the piano, what's a sharp and what's a flat, and where G is on the score. These are basic things, but most of all, she taught me how to enjoy playing those old great (and simple) American songs like *Beautiful Dreamer*, *Shenandoah*, and *Yankee Doodle*—treasures from the great American songbook. They are easy to learn if you know the lyrics and know simple chords and if you put in some work (yes, work, if you pardon the expression) at the piano. Picture yourself impressing friends, relatives, and parents by playing these gems from memory or by sight-reading.

PIANO BY HEART

Hey! Would it surprise you to know that most musicians in the world neither sight-read nor play from memory? They play only by ear. If you can play by ear, more power to you. But playing from memory and sight-reading will also increase your playing power by large amounts and make you a happier, more contented pianist.

Miss Platz did not believe in recitals. So, with her, there were none. The only other student I ever heard play was the brown-noser girl whose lesson was ahead of mine. At the end of eight years (age six to 14) at the piano, Miss Platz told my mother that I had no talent for music and that there was no sense in continuing lessons.

Attention! Here is an important lesson: Insulate yourself from creative injury that is all too often inflicted on children who are music students.

I was not offended by Miss Platz's revelation, and neither was my mother. It did not hurt me. There was no need to genuflect. I did not suffer a severe creative injury as some helicopter mothers told me was inflicted on their child. This truth did not change my sense of self. It was the truth, and truth is hard to contradict. No, change that. Truth is impossible to contradict. After eight years at the piano, I was not yet halfway through my first-year piano book. Something was wrong. My brain was not big enough. My hand coordination was not good enough. I had trouble seeing the notes. Who knows what the problem was? No matter how hard I tried, most of the pieces were simply beyond my ability at the time. So, that was that. Meanwhile, I continued to amuse myself by sight-reading the old standard American songs. If you are interested, I recommend *The American Song Treasury: 100 Favorites* by Theodore Raph, Dover Books on Popular Music, Mineola, New York.

Sidebar About Musical Talent

Yes, I have no talent for music. So what! I think most musicians will agree that most of their playing is not due to any intrinsic talent for music. Instead, it derives directly from hard work. Stevie Wonder, in a personal interview with the psychologist Daniel J. Levitin (Music and Mind, edited by Renée Fleming, Viking 2024, page 23), stated that the key is holding on to and nurturing what is. Stevie recalled the thousands, possibly tens of thousands, of hours of hard work he had put into nurturing and that it didn't come easy or naturally. Stevie believes musical ability is the result of lots of practice. And that should tell us something.

Teacher Two: Madge Hunt taught me the supreme importance of the score. The score, she said, is the Talmud of music memory. Jews and Christians believe in the sacredness of the Bible, so as a performing musician, you should consider the written score as being sacred. It is sacred as it represents the piece as it emerged from the composer, the creator. You must have the score as your reference when memorizing because one memorizes consciously and unconsciously not only the notes and chords but the general organization, the color, shapes, and positions of items and what the top, bottom, and middle look like. Unconsciously, your brain is also memorizing the environment in which you are developing your memory of a piece, including the temperature of the room, the general quality of the air, local smells, and many other factors you may not be consciously aware of.

Advice: Use only one score per piece.

Review this one and only copy of the score to see if in fact you have mastered the piece. Review and repeated testing of your performance is the most secure way to a good performance. If you use different copies of the same score, your memory task will be harder, and your brain will be confused.

Repeat Memory Rule

When you are working to memorize a particular piece, always use the same score. The familiar face of it and the organization will help cement your memory. The written score, and only the written score, makes verbatim playing possible. Switching to a different score of the same piece will do nothing but cause trouble and confusion. Confusion is the mother of ignorance and forgetfulness, but orderly arrangement helps intelligent analysis and firms up memory. Stick with the same score until the piece is fully memorized and a part of you. Try to play the same way every time. Be particular about fingering, articulations, and any details of performance. The human brain likes repetitive patterns of behavior, which we call habits. Once you develop a habit about a certain piece, you will play it automatically (or almost automatically), just the way you tie your shoelaces automatically. About other memory tricks to help you memorize and deal with the score, more later.

Madge also taught me music theory (grades one through ten with written exams). To me, music theory was not boring. Au contraire—learning music theory opened a whole new world of understanding harmony and form, both of which are important to memorization. From a simple refrain form (like a ritornello) to bigger concepts like sonata form, it is important to know how your music is constructed. Harmonic analysis goes a long way in the learning process, so don't be afraid to use one of your practice sessions to map out exactly how your piece is put together. The more you understand your music intellectually, the better you will play it and the easier it will be to memorize.

Madge taught scales and arpeggios because she believed in that sort of training. It is helpful to know how to play a C major scale correctly by dipping the thumb under to play the F. Starting with C, the correct fingering is 123123412312345 for two octaves. That way you don't run out of fingers. Other scales may have little tricks that adapt to their situation on the keyboard. Worry about that stuff if and when you come across it.

Every scale is the same spacing, which resembles C major, namely whole note, whole note, half note, whole note, whole note, whole note, half. Abbreviated WWHWWWH or 00/000/. In my view, scales and arpeggios will be better worked on if and when they are part of the piece at hand. Otherwise, I consider work on scales a waste of time—time that could have been better spent learning and mastering a desired piece of music for fun and pleasure. When you spend time on scales and such, you incur an opportunity cost. The time you spend could have been spent doing something more productive and more fun. Think about this point. It's important.

Madge was the only teacher of mine who examined my fingernails to make sure the nails were properly trimmed and short enough so that they would not produce clicking on the piano. That was good advice. Trim your fingernails short enough so they don't click.

Madge taught all the chords. Plus, with her, there was occasional training in rhythm using bongo drums, and there was what she called ear training. During ear training, she sounded a chord and asked if it was major or minor. She would sound two notes and ask what the interval was between them. Usually, I got the difference between major and minor because the minor sounded sad, but on the other tasks of ear training, I was hopeless.

Madge liked the idea of counting and the use of the metronome. I do not approve of either. If you play with a metronome or count the beats for any time, it tends to ruin your feeling for the emotional content of the music, which is the vital expression I aimed for. Madge said my playing should be as regular as a heartbeat. Ho ho ho. As a physician, I know the heartbeats are not regular; they vary with respiration, which itself is often irregular with pauses and sighs. The only people who have absolutely regular heartbeats are those who have pacemakers. The only people who have a uniform pattern of respiration are the dead because they are not breathing at all.

Sidebar About Synchronization and Entrainment

These are important items for ensemble playing but not really needed by soloists. All humans synchronize. For example, we synchronize our internal biological clock to actual systemic, external time cues from ticking clocks. We calibrate sleep and wake cycles based on rhythmic changes in light and darkness, morning and night. And I play musical phrases according to my breathing cycle and not according to the strict timing demanded by Madge. Poets do not recite in strict time. Their performance varies with how they feel and how they handle the pauses and caesuras. If you look at Grieg's *Butterfly* or his *To Spring*—to play these correctly, in my view, you need to synchronize and desynchronize throughout the piece just as happens in the natural events and things Grieg is trying to emulate and copy. In fact, Grieg gives specific instructions on what he thinks should be slowed or speeded and when to get back to the original tempo. Don't believe me? Look at the last page of *To Spring*. Here's what you will find: cresc. molto, sosten. rit. a tempo dim. e poco a poco. piu rit. Lento. A street piano, mechanical and tired, cannot possibly follow such directions, but you can, and by doing so, you can bring the music alive and make it a more interesting marker of our fluid identity.

By the way, there is natural synchronization in the material universe. An example of this in a nonbiological system comes from the 17th-century scientist Christiaan Huygens, who demonstrated that pairs of moving pendulums become synchronized independent of human physical intervention.

Recital

Madge was very big on recitals, so we had many of them. Preparation of the piece was hard work and was done over several weeks and sometimes over months until it met her high standard—absolute correct tempo, no wrong notes, exact duplication of the score. Madge selected the pieces and drilled them into me.

Recital competition was stiff, especially from the child prodigies of Asian descent, but I managed to get 19 trophies because I had worked very hard to master pieces like *To a Wild Rose* by Edward MacDowell, *Fur Elise* by Ludwig Van Beethoven, and *Prelude in A major, no. 7 in Opus 28* by Chopin. I put in at least 160 hours memorizing and perfecting *Fur Elise* before Madge would let me enter it in competition. I fell in love with the prelude, a brief simple masterpiece. To this day, before I start each practice session, I play the Chopin prelude, first from memory and then from notes, and discover deeper and deeper levels of beauty in it. It is a flawless work, timeless and immortal, that lies well within the technical grasp of every serious amateur. The more intimately we know our pieces, the more we value them. The more I play the Chopin prelude, the more I appreciate its depth of character and its worth. In the nest volume of this book, we will discuss how to play and how to memorize Chopin's prelude. And we will work *on Fur Elise*.

I won some competitions because I had worked hard, and the judges liked my freer, nonrobotic playing of the old masterpieces. The kids I was competing against were supportive, and many gave thumbs up after I performed. The usual comment from them was "Today you played better than usual." Usually before I played my piece, I announced to the judges and to the audience, "I am here to make the kids look good."

My nemesis came one Saturday morning at San Jacinto Junior College when I played Mozart's *Menuetto* from *First Viennese Sonatina*. With Madge, I played it straight and got on the program. But then, for some reason known only to God, I decided to ad lib and have some fun. In my view, Mozart had attention deficit disorder and liked to play around with his music. So, before the audience and the two judges, I played my own (rather loose, freer, imaginative, and capricious) interpretation of the piece with a few wrong notes, incorrect dynamics, and multiple slips. Amazingly, there were lots of applause, but none from Madge.

Madge was irate and screamed at me in the hallway. "I am ashamed to be your teacher! How can anyone as intelligent as you not know how to play Mozart? You have a brilliant memory, but are sloppy in its application. You have no talent for music. The only thing that saves you is you love music."

A week went by, and Madge gave me the written appraisal of one of the judges. He loved my version and praised it to the sky. Madge said she wouldn't give me the other judge's appraisal "because it will give you a swelled head." And then she handed me the Mozart Trophy. I said, "Madge, how come if my playing was so bad, I won the trophy?" Madge: "The judges felt sorry for you because you're an old man."

So, what was the lesson? Different people have different ideas about what is good and what is not. We have to learn to accept that fact, and we have to learn to accept rejection or disapproval when it comes our way. My ego is such (gigantic, really) that adverse criticisms wash off my shoulders like rainwater. When you get an adverse opinion, try to find out why. If the criticism makes sense, then pay attention to the item during the next performance. If the criticism does not make sense to you or doesn't seem helpful, forget it.

Let's give Madge the credit she is due. Thanks, Madge. Without you, I would not know the basics—familiarity with the elemental material of music: scales, chords, measure, and rhythm. You did not cover the principles of harmonic progression, analysis of music design, conventional outlines of form which tend to reveal the order and tonality of certain styles of music. Some of those were covered on the written tests. Other teachers will expand on that, and much of it I would learn on my own.

Madge, you were a good teacher for me at the time, but the work became too onerous, and there wasn't enough fun. And there were too many recitals, so I decided to bow out and get another teacher.

OK. True confession: the main reason I left Madge was I didn't like the way she marked up all my musical scores. In my view, the score had all the information I needed, and it was not necessary to circle the tempo to remind me what that was, and it was not necessary to mark each note with what finger she thought should play it, and it was not necessary to mark the counts 1&2&3&4& on each and every measure, and so forth. Give me a clean unmarked score, and I am happy and at home. In the bibliography at the end of this book, you will find lots of books written by very capable teachers who say you should mark up your score in detail to help you master and memorize the piece. That is peachy for some people, but some people ain't me. I like a nice clean score, and I don't want anyone marking it up, not even myself. When you get the urge to scribble on your score, think how you could just memorize what you are about to note and how much better it will be to train yourself to memorize those things instead of marking them. The more you train your memory, the better it will get. Many neurologists, myself included, view writing as an enemy of memory. But I do admit there are some people whose memory benefits from actually writing things down, like the chord progression and bass notes. If writing helps you, then do it. But don't do it too much. Trust your memory instead.

Later, you will see that I violate this rule about writing on the score. I did this for instructional purposes. Einstein said consistency is not a human trait. And Camus said, "The absurd man is he who doesn't change." Change if you must to suit the circumstances, and don't change if it doesn't help. I believe an amateur pianist should be free and flexible, and I practice what I preach.

Parting from Madge was such sweet sorrow. In a note, she thanked me for being her student and said I had given her great pleasure as a teacher, and she was proud of the progress I had made. After reading that, I felt like crying. Boy, was I a heel! But it was too late to reverse course. As a consolation, I sent Madge a bouquet of flowers.

Sidebar About Basics

Without a basic understanding of chords that Madge taught, you will be significantly handicapped in memorizing your pieces. Scales are not half as important as chords, so you can neglect scales and concentrate attention on chords. Learn to quickly identify chords as whole units and not as individual letters. Just as when reading, you would identify the whole word and not the individual letters that make up the word. You would not read H-O-U-S-E. You would instantly read and recognize the word house. Try for the same instant recognition of chords.

How about we work on chords right now? Let's get them firmly in mind so we can use them as tools to vastly improve our playing, our fun, and our ability to memorize pieces.

Chords

Three or more notes sounded together are what is usually considered a chord. The basic chords are major and minor, diminished, and augmented. If you know the configuration of C major, C minor, C diminished, and C augmented, you can easily play (by copying the configuration) any major, minor, diminished, or augmented chord.

C major is CEG with a major third between the C and E and a minor third between the E and G. If you don't know what a major third or a minor third is, don't worry. You can just count off the semitones. Start with C, go up a semitone to C#, then hit the next note, which is D, and then D# followed by E. It took four semitones to get to the middle note E. Now check this out: It takes three semitones to get from E to G. They are F, F#, and G. Bingo! That's all there is to it.

All major chords will consist of a major third followed by a minor third—four semitones followed by three semitones. Practice this on the piano. Put your thumb on an F# and sound F# major. Having trouble? Count it out. From F#, go to G, then G#, then A, then A#. Therefore, the middle tone of F# major is A#. Count off again to find the end tone is C#. Put your thumb on any key and sound the major. Do G major, F major, D major, and so forth. Once you know the formula, all the majors come easy. Practice the chords, especially C, G, and F major, which play major roles in piano pieces.

I am not looking at you right now, but I would bet that, like the average reader, you would find the practice of chords too boring, and you will not do it. Mental laziness accounts for a great deal of the lack of progress in this wide world, especially in complex disciplines like piano playing. Hard work is the key to success in any endeavor, be it chess, business, music, neurosurgery, skydiving, and so forth. Hard work and production of goods and services is the major way most Americans avoid poverty.

Work at the piano should be fun, and it is necessary for achievement.

Choose! Would you like to swing on a star? Carry moonbeams home in a jar and be better off than you are? Or would you rather be a fish? A fish won't do anything but swim in a brook. He can't write his name or read a book.

Back to Chords

Minor chords are easy too. They are a minor third followed by a major third. So, to convert a major chord to a minor, we lower the middle tone by a semitone. Pretty cool! Right?

Thus, C minor is C-Eb-G. F# minor would be F#-A-C#.

Diminished chords consist of two minor thirds. C diminished would be made by lowering the G in C minor a semitone to get C-Eb-Gb. F# diminished would be made by lowering the C# to C in F# minor. Later we will discuss the trick of recognizing diminished chords as part of one three or four-note diminished chord.

Augmented chords consist of two major thirds. They are not so important because they are rarely used. To make an augmented chord, just raise note five of the triad by a semitone. C augmented would be C-E-G#. G augmented would be G-B-D#.

Seven chords just add a minor third to the triad chord to make a 7th chord. If we add a major third to the triad, we get a major seventh, which is nowhere as popular as the regular minor 7th. Try to get familiar with the way seventh chords look and feel. Once you have mastered the chords, including seventh chords, you will be able to play any simple fake book piece and make pretty good music. In fact, at this point, I suggest you invest in a fake book. Amazon has many for sale. Start with the easiest in C major, and you will have a barrel of fun and improve your sight-reading at the same time. No kidding. Fake books will be good for you. Lots of fun and nice practice playing familiar well-loved songs. Recommended: *The Easy Jazz Standards Fake Book* (get the one in the key of C) Hal Leonard, Milwaukee. Also get: *Your First Fake Book*, Hal Leonard.

Whoa! You might at this point be wondering what a fake book is and why Doctor Patten (Doctor Patten is me, the person writing the stuff in this book. I am the person addressing you directly) is suggesting you get one.

What Is a Fake Book?

A fake book (also known as a lead sheet) is one of the most useful tools for musicians, amateur and professional alike. A fake book has just a single line of music, similar to the right hand in standard piano music. To make it even simpler, there is only one melody note at a time. There are symbols consisting of letters and numbers above the musical notes, such as Cm, B7, etc. These symbols provide flexible guides for creating chords, giving you the freedom to play at whatever level of difficulty you wish. Believe it or not, the fake book has allowed me virtually unlimited freedom to be creative and at the same time have fun impressing people by playing some of the best-loved and most-requested standards. Try it!

Quiz time: What does G7 look like?
Answer: GBDF or BDFG or DFGB or FGBD

What does Cm above the melody note in a fake book suggest?
Answer: Play a C minor chord with that note.

What does F7 look like? At the piano, play it in all its forms.
Answer: FACD#—any combination. The F7 I like the best is CD#FA because it fits my hand nicely.
FACE would not be F7—it is F major 7.

Practice making C7, A7, and E7 as they appear quite often in popular music. Try to recognize them as easily as you recognize the words cat, dog, man, fish, and house.

Here's a list of the usual chords as usually abbreviated:
C = C major chord
Cm = C minor chord
Cm6 = minor 6th chord (C minor with the 6th note attached, in this case A)
Cm7 = minor 7th chord
C7 = 7th chord
C+ = C augmented
C7+ = 7th augmented
Co = C diminished (usually a diminished with three or four notes)

The other chords follow the same pattern. F = F major chord; Fm = F minor, etc.

More on Chords

When a chord is arranged in its most compact form containing only thirds (like C major above—CEG), the lowest pitch is the root and is sometimes labeled I, the Roman numeral for one. Note five is sometimes labeled V, the Roman numeral for five, and the fourth note (guess what) is labeled IV. Western music is very big on the relations of I and V and IV, as you probably know already. Most students are taught the cadences that work from the I chord to IV to V (or V7). Cadences come in handy sometimes when you blank out. Just play the cadences and hope you regain your memory footing.

Any actual chord can be altered into different configurations and still remain the same chord because it has the same letters. Let's shift the C and see what happens. Moving the C up to the next higher C, we get EGC, which is called the first inversion, and GCE the second inversion. It's the same chord with the same notes just spread out differently. Get used to recognizing the chords in their different positions. That will help your sight-reading and will also make memorizing easier.

CHORDS AS A CHUNKING TOOL

◆ ◆ ◆

A chord is any set of three or more different notes on the piano. Each item in the definition is important. There must be a set, that is an assemblage or collection of notes. There must be at least three notes. And those notes must be different. Go to the piano and play the following examples. Tell which are chords and which are not chords.

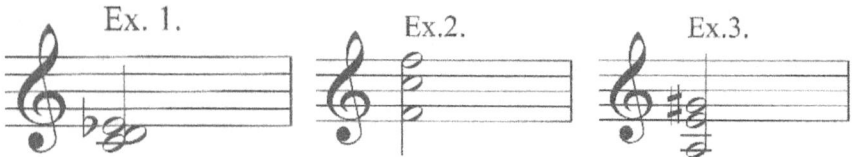

Only two of these are chords. Look at example two. It has an F and a C and another F. This is three notes—but not three different notes. It takes three DIFFERENT notes to make a chord. So, example two is not a chord. By the way, notice that the example that was not a chord was by far the best sounding of the three examples.

Thinking and Tinkering Time

O.K., are you still at the piano? Randomly select three or more notes and play them together. It probably sounds horrible. In fact, you could sit at the piano all day playing three or more random notes together and find that most of them sound like the music for a grade "B" horror movie. Thank goodness, the great musicians and composers of the past have already tried every possible combination and have arrived at a general agreement on the four specific types of chords that sound good or okay.

The 88 notes of the piano represent to me the entire pitch range of human voices, from soprano to bass. When these pitches are activated randomly, it does sound horrible to some people. But others can be impressed. There was a funny movie I remember where the guy, out for seduction, takes the babe back to his apartment and starts pounding on the keys. She says, "Oh, you are playing Schoenberg so well," and he says, "I can do this all day. I'm just pounding random notes."

To me, this random set of notes reflects not the great mathematical order of the universe that Plato and Pythagoras envisioned, but the cosmic cacophony, the essential chaotic wholeness from which the musical artists and composers draw form, order, and beauty.

My son, Craig, has a cat that likes to step on the keys of the piano. The sounds produced are pretty random. When my wife, Ethel, hears modern atonal music, she calls it cat music because, to her, that is the way it sounds. Our lesson: avoid sounding like a cat on the keys. Stick with the chords that sound good.

Chord Styles

Chords are played in many patterns or styles. These styles fall into two main categories: Blocks and Arpeggios.

Block Chords

Block chords occur when all three or more notes of the chord are played somewhere on the piano at the same time. Sometimes they are laid out in a simple pattern, easy to recognize, and sometimes they are laid out in a complex pattern and are not easy to recognize.

Note: For a group of notes to be considered a chord, it must contain three different notes. If a group of notes does not have three different notes, it is not a chord, even if it sounds pleasing. For example, a group with duplicate notes (e.g., C-C-E) is not a chord. Interestingly, such combinations can sometimes sound better than actual chords.

Ex. 4.

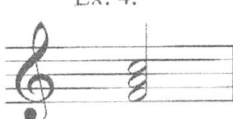

Did you recognize that this is a major chord in the root position? If not, then you have some work to do because you are seriously behind the power curve. Memorizing each of the major chords in the root position such that you can instantly recognize them will help you chunk chords and will facilitate music memory.

Answer: The chord is F Major

How about the next chord? What is it?

PIANO BY HEART

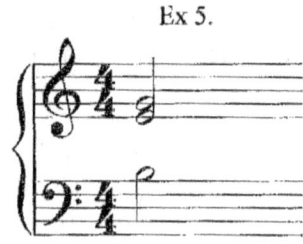

Ex 5.

Music Detective Work

This chord requires a little detective work. Music detectives keep in mind that the musical alphabet is made up of only seven letters: A, B, C, D, E, F, G. At this point, you might try to memorize the letters of the musical alphabet and the order in which they are written. (Only kidding, of course. If you didn't know the alphabet up to and including G, you wouldn't be able to read this book.)

Major and minor chords are made of every other letter of the musical alphabet, so the combination that makes up chords is harder to think about because we originally memorized the alphabet in the exact order of letters and not in the order of every other letter. This is the reason ABC comes to us pretty much automatically, whereas ACE (A minor) or GBD (G major) doesn't. With that in mind, let's look again at example 5. It's BEG.

BEG can't be a B chord because in a B chord we expect some kind of D (natural or sharp) followed by some kind of F (natural or sharp). BD#F# is B major, one of my favorite chords. BDF# would be B minor. Still awake? Still with me? If so, play these on the piano.

OK, good. Now we know what BEG is not. Let's find out what it is.

To discover the root note of the chord and therefore the name of the chord, we must mentally rearrange the notes into a sequence of every other letter of the musical alphabet, recognizing that when we get to G, the musical alphabet starts again at A. So, the crucial question is how do you arrange BEG into an every-other-letter sequence?

We can't see you out there, but we know that most of you have figured out that the sequence must be EGB and that this is some kind of E chord. Play this on the piano if you need to. Actually playing the notes and the chord in the root position and in the BEG sequence will help you to remember what's going on because you will be seeing it, feeling it, hearing it, doing it, and thinking about it. Can you think of any other arrangement of this chord? Answer: GBE.

By the way, what is the name of the chord?
Answer: E minor

Try your detective skills on the next example, naming each note:

Ex.6.

This example requires some thinking. Arrange the notes in every other letter sequence. Here are the answers:

The letter names are from bottom up: D G D Bb

The correct letter sequence is: G B D

The root of the chord is: G

Therefore, this is some kind of G chord. Play this chord in sequence on the piano and match it up with what you know about the types of chords. Discover what formula matches what you are playing. It is a G minor chord: G Bb D.

Ta-da! You have just done chord analysis. You will see in our memory work that we will be taking notice of chords to provide easy chunking memory tools. It is much easier to remember "E major chord" than it is to remember E E at octave in the left hand and G# in the right thumb, middle finger on B and pinky on the top E, for the idea of E major will remind you of E and B and G#, giving you a better chance at recalling what to play and where to play it. Thus, chords are memory tools, for they often help reduce a series of notes into a simpler, often single definable entity, which is easier to recall.

Full disclosure: Early on, I decided to memorize the chord alphabet so that I almost automatically can recite ACE, BDF, CEG, DFA, EGB, FAC, GBD. If I have trouble with recalling any sequence, I just refer to my mental image of the notes on the piano keyboard. I visualize myself starting to play the first note and then I see in my mind's eye the other two notes that must make up the chord. Once I see those notes, I can name them. Identifying chords by name helps a lot, especially initially with your piano work. Later you will just automatically recognize the chords and play them pretty much automatically. Those of you who touch type know your fingers automatically hit the correct key without conscious thought. The same can happen eventually with piano playing if you stick with it long enough.

It might be a good idea to stop here and memorize the patterns and practice making chords of all four varieties. These chords are one of the foundations of music. They are so important we will review their construction again later.

The names of the chords are not as important as the patterns of the chords, and the patterns of the chords are not as important as your ability to play the chords.

How Many Types of Chords Are There?

In Western music, there are only 31 types of chords. Remember this fact by recalling the number of flavors in Baskin-Robbins ice cream: 31 flavors.

Major chords—twelve notes to start, therefore twelve chords. Some chords are enharmonic duplications, the same exact chords made from the same exact notes. For instance, F# Major is the same chord as Gb Major because F# and Gb are the same pitch.

Minor chords—twelve notes to start, therefore twelve chords. Some chords are enharmonic duplications (same pitch different name) as discussed above. Ab minor is the same chord as G# minor, as Ab and G# are the same pitch.

That reminds me. What do you get when you drop a piano down a mine shaft? Answer: A flat miner.

Get it?
Sorry!

Augmented chords—only four possible. Work this out on the keyboard if you are feeling ambitious. Trust me if you are not feeling ambitious. OK just for your reference here are the four augmented chords:

CEG# C#FA DF#A# D#GB

Remember each of the notes in the augmented chord can appear in a different order just like the notes in major and minor chords. Thus, CEG# can be EG#C and G#CE.

Diminished chords—only three possible chords to encompass all twelve notes if you are playing four notes at a time as explained. Start with the root note and go up by minor thirds. Do C and then do C# and then do D. When you get to D# you will note you are repeating a diminished chord you already played except the notes are in a different position. Just for the record, here is the chord speller for diminished chords. I would memorize these by their position and configurations on the keyboard. I would not memorize them by their letters. Knowing them well by keyboard position will come in handy and will help your memory tasks.

CD#F#A C#EGA# DFG#B

Adding things up, we get: 12 Majors, 12 minors, four augmented, three diminished (four notes) for a grand total of $12 + 12 + 4 + 3 = 31$. Hence, 31 chords that sound good or sound okay.

Arpeggios

At times a composer will take a chord and spread it out by playing one note at a time instead of sounding all the notes of the chord together. Go to the piano and play the C major chord (CEG) not as a block of notes but as individual notes sounded separately. Keep the right pedal down when you do this so that the piano will keep the sound of all three notes when you have finished sounding each. Play the C major chord as a block note. Does it sound the same as the arpeggio? The style is different, but the sound is, with the pedal down, fundamentally the same.

Now try this. Look at the next example and do some detective work. This is the first measure of the Bach Prelude No. 28 in C Major from *Notebook for Anna Magdalena Bach*. There are more than three notes, but the notes you are looking at are part of one chord. What's its name?

Ex. 7

28.

Did you get it? It's the C major chord all over again, a fancy version to be sure, but a C major chord nevertheless. While we are doing some thinking about this famous piece by Bach, let's go ahead and look at the next two measures. Identifying this next chord will be tricky.

Ex. 8

If you put the notes in every other letter order, it spells D F A C. Now before you yell, I know that this doesn't match any one of the four patterns discussed earlier. It doesn't, and in a way, it does. It is actually a D chord (D F A) with an added note. The added note is C.

Composers like to play around with the four basic chord types and add extra notes to find an interesting sound, a unique sound, a specific color, or just something a little different from the ordinary major and minor chords that make up the vast percentage of Western music.

No problem. The D chord is still a chunking tool, and I shall just recall what needs to be played by saying this is a D chord with a C attached.

It is still possible to find the core chord by using the every other letter spelling of the notes. FAC also seems possible, though less desirable as a chunking tool as here F A C is an F chord with a D attached. Actually, as a chunking tool, this makes some sense to me because D is the relative minor of F major.

If there is a situation where we can't make all the notes line up in every other letter sequence, then play the notes together leaving out one note at a time until you get to a note that doesn't seem to change the basic sound of the chord. In the D F# A C chord, see if you don't agree that leaving the C out makes the chord sound like a major chord, which, not incidentally, it is. Now play the D minor chord and add a C on top. What did you get? D minor 7! That could be your chunking tool for this Bach piece.

Test yourself with combinations like this. This method requires a good ear for chords that some people don't have. A good ear for chords can develop with time, but probably not by the time that you finish this book. As with everything else, you will get better with focused attention to the problem and practice. This next example comes from the famous Bach Cello Suite No. 1.

Ex. 9

In these measures, there are Gs, Ds, Bs, and an A. There is no way to put these four notes into every other letter order, but you can put three of them in the correct order: GBD, the G major chord. The A is an add-on. Prove this by playing the following as block chords:

GBD
GAB (ugh!)
GAD (ugh!)
ABD (ugh!)

No combination of these four notes sounds as good as GBD. So, throw out the A and you have the root chord.

It is interesting how one solves the chord problem musically and by analysis. As for me, I go by the preponderant weight of evidence. Here, the four notes have embedded in them the G major chord—no question about that—so that must be the root chord. But even if it were not the root chord, imagining that it is the root chord would work just as well because the notes I need to remember are GBD. If I had some other way of organizing the notes in my memory that worked as well as a chord chunk, then I might use that. For instance, I might tell myself that there is an A thrown in here on top of a G major chord for a reason. A is the dominant note of the D major chord, and D is the fifth note of the G major chord. The relation between fifths is very important in Western music, such that the fifth above the top note (D) of the G chord leads to the A in question by a fifth. In fact, some books would call this relation secondary dominance. Whether this analysis makes sense or not, it doesn't much matter if the narration and the analysis help me recall what to play and when. It was Bach who said, when he was complimented on his organ playing, that there wasn't much to it: "You just play the right notes at the right time."

I hope this introduction to chords will help you chunk notes together and will help you more readily follow the music memory methods. Over time, recognizing the chord structure of music will also help you see how composers use chords. Certain patterns, habits of expression, and favorite sound combinations are unique to each of the great masters. Knowing these and recognizing these will make future pieces by the same composer more understandable. It is a very fulfilling moment when you look at a piece by Beethoven and you can say to yourself, "There he goes again." A lifelong study of chords will bring that kind of understanding to your musicianship. Maybe someday I'll write a book about the tricks and patterns of the great composers.

Scales

Scale recognition is also a chunking tool that helps music memory. A scale is a pattern sequence of notes that sound good. Somehow scales harness a musical force that causes one of the notes of the scale to sound like the home note. This home note makes the scale complete; ending on any other note makes the sequence sound unfinished. Prove this to yourself by going to the piano and playing the following sequence:

CDEFGAB

That's right. Stop and hold that last B. Do you feel the frustration? Doesn't it sound like something is missing? Doesn't it sound like something is not finished?

OK, you have tortured yourself enough. Go ahead and play the next note, which is C again.

Aaah! That's more like it. Relief at last!

Play again the whole sequence (CDEFGABC) while listening to how the sequence of notes sounds complete right after you hit that higher C. Now play them backward. Start on the top C and work down. Same effect. The backward play is called an inversion because the sequence is played in reverse order, a situation called (in music) inverted.

In this scale, C is the home note that makes the scale sound complete. Let's do a quick analysis of this scale and discover the pattern for the major scales of which the C major scale can be the prototype pattern (remember?) WWHWWWH or 00/000/.

Teacher Three: Jimmy White

Jimmy White has developed his own piano course consisting of classical pieces that get more and more complex. The emphasis was on sight-reading and not looking at the keyboard. Jimmy is not much concerned about wrong notes. He is interested in the overall effect and whether the piece has been played musically. Hard to say what he meant by musically, but more or less, I think he means putting the human touch on the performance and not sounding like a robot. Humans vary dynamics and make some attempts at showing emotion and even expressing personality. Many finer shadings and dynamic differences are up to the interpreter—namely you. Termination of phrases to convey the idea that one must separate the end of the melody somewhat before proceeding with what follows is up to the interpreter—namely you. In my view, if these little pauses are not observed, people of taste will find that something is missing in the execution. In short, this is the difference between those who read without interruption and those who stop at periods and commas. Meaningful phrasing remains as important for the performance of music as it does for reciting poetry or delivering the news on CNN.

"Forget wrong notes. Play on!" Jimmy was quoting Franz Liszt. And we listened to famous composers play their own pieces and make multiple mistakes, yet the overall effect was good. This was particularly true with Claude Debussy, who made many errors of rhythm and pitch while playing his own masterpieces.

Scott Joplin never made an audio recording, but in 1916, he made seven piano rolls of his masterpiece "Maple Leaf Rag." In my view, the available rolls are pumped too fast in the mistaken belief that ragtime should be played fast. Joplin, in his essay *School of Ragtime—6 Exercises for Piano,* says three times, "ragtime should never be played fast."

Joplin's playing is disorganized and poor. One critic said it was "distressing to hear." Joplin misses the cadences in part one, gets sloppy in part two with many wrong notes, forgets to repeat part three in Db major, and generally fouls up the interesting melody of part four. If he had been in recital at the time, the judges would have given him a class three, the lowest grade. Perhaps the syphilis that would kill him the following year was interfering with the proper execution of his own masterpiece, or perhaps he was just another one of those composers who have trouble playing their own compositions.

YouTube has a nice video of Kurt Weill singing and playing his 1934 timeless masterpiece *Speak Low*. He is not a singer, and he makes mistakes on the piano, but the overall effect is interesting and worth listening to.

Check out Edvard Grieg playing his *To Spring* (Op. 43, No. 6). His version is unusual. Note that he completely omits the repeat of section one and doesn't seem to stretto on measure five of section two. His version differs from the four others I listened to on YouTube. His playing is good, but he didn't follow the rules that most teachers would enforce. If he can do that, why can't we? Compare and contrast Grieg's version (1903), which lasts one minute and 53 seconds, with Lang Lang's version, which lasts three minutes and 59 seconds. Quite a difference! And yet both are excellent. Both these artists move outside expected patterns of thinking and look at the same piece from a new perspective. If artists can't freely do this, freely express themselves, who can?

Lesson: Personal Style and Expression

Don't be afraid to add your personal style to the pieces you play. Untapped potential is a drain on your future achievements and humanity's bounty. That is my lived experience. Justifying it on a scientific level is a different matter. You decide! Am I right or wrong?

Making Different Sounds with the Same Note

Jimmy showed me how to make a single note sound different depending on where and how you pressed it. He could make six different sounds from middle C. No kidding. I learned to make three tones on the same key. This expands the kind of sound color you can use at performance. I learned to press the keys with a large area of my fingers holding them parallel (not perpendicular) to the keyboard, producing a nice mellow sound which became my signature. Experiment with different articulations and see what you like and don't like.

Jimmy tried to develop my composition powers by playing a little game. You may wish to try the same. He would assign a story or ask me to make up a story and then, using that story, compose a musical piece. It's fun and interesting and has given me much pleasure and quite a bit of piano experience, especially at the upper and lower registers where the usual composer fears to tread. Recently, I played my own piece entitled *Callie and Shai Among the Wildflowers,* based on what I saw when my two granddaughters, Callie and Shai, wandered among wildflowers. When I played my piece, my wife Ethel shouted from her study: "Wow! What's that? I haven't heard that before or anything like it—very nice." From this kind of play, I got the idea of tap dancing to the rhythms of famous poems and I did a few demonstrations for Jimmy and made a YouTube video to Shakespeare's three witch scene: "When shall we three witches meet again? In thunder, lightning or in rain," etc. Jimmy was amused but thought I should concentrate more on music composition since it was more complex and required more concentration, and he said for me, duplicating the rhythms of famous poems with my tap shoes was too easy.

Jimmy doesn't believe in recitals, so with him as teacher, the heat was off. It's just sight-reading every lesson. Occasionally, Jimmy would show a trick. He showed me if you use four notes, then there are only three kinds of diminished chords and all the diminished chords are part of those three as we discussed above. Did you work on these? I hope so. Knowledge of diminished chords will come in handy when and if you memorize *Piano Concerto in A Minor* by Edvard Grieg.

Quiz Time: Put your hand on F diminished.
Answer: F G# B or G# B F or B F G#

Along the way, Jimmy seemed to get tired of teaching. He seemed to become less patient with wrong notes or errors in rhythm, and he seemed to be especially unhappy with young kids who obviously failed to prepare for the lesson or who had trouble reading the score. Jimmy said he sometimes caught himself screaming at a kid who was staring at G4 and couldn't figure out what note he (the student) was looking at.

Jimmy had gigs where he played at various parties for corporations and private parties, and I think he also had jobs at local churches as a music director. So, his enthusiasm for teaching waned, and I believe he suffered from burnout.

One day I asked him if he was concerned about the progress or the lack of progress of his students. He said he didn't care as long as they paid his fee ($100/hour, but he always taught me at a discount $80/hour. I never asked why I got the discount, but I did.).

And then I asked if he was concerned about my progress or lack of progress. He said he didn't really care as long as I continued to pay his fee.

Jimmy told me about a new teacher in our area and suggested I might apply to her for lessons. He didn't actually say I had no talent for music, but it looked like that was what he believed. So, I bowed out because I wanted a teacher who cared about my progress or lack of progress.

Teacher Four: Ying Zhang

Ying has multiple degrees in music, including a Doctorate in Performing Arts from Rice University, a degree I consider equivalent to completing a residency in neurosurgery. She is light on recitals—two a year, one in June and one in December. She is easygoing and nowhere as intense as Madge. Fundamentally, I love Ying. She was just right for me and had no qualms about supervising my playing popular songs as well as pieces from the classical repertoire. With Ying, there is no ear training, no Hannon, no practice scales, no bongo drums—just concentration on pieces and having fun with them.

Of course, Ying never once marked up my music. She would point out things in the score and would suggest fingering and correct rhythms, but she did not mark the score. My memory is good enough to get what she wanted fixed, and I didn't need a marked-up score to remind me. By the way, in preparation to write this book, I read dozens of books about advice to musicians. Most suggest you mark up your score as a reminder of various things. My advice is, as I said before, DON'T DO IT. If you need written reminders, put them on a separate paper and keep your score clean. In the future, when you review a piece, a clean score will usually serve you better than a marked-up one.

My lessons with Ying stopped during the pandemic but have restarted once a week. The pandemic was helpful: It gave me time to read books on memory and music, and it gave me time to write.

In my opinion, Ying is not a good teacher. She is a great teacher with lots of experience. Her relaxed, humane enthusiasm for music serves the students well, often counterpointing and sometimes contradicting received systems of thought while attaching to broader ideas. In some places, Ying and I may not see eye to eye. But we, as student and teacher, are not afraid to grapple with the untidy realities of teaching and learning. My problem is with tempo, and Ying knows it. I just can't play as fast as others or as people expect a piece to be played. Thank God, Ying is usually OK with that. And so, you, dear reader, would do well to get a kind of teacher who is OK with Socratic rational dialogue and not into dogma. With a flexible approach to music learning, you will then judge which view, which ideas, which reasons are more cogent, more likely to be true, and under what conditions and circumstances, and, most importantly, which actually apply to you.

Sidebar About Selecting (and Deselecting) a Teacher

Be picky but not too picky about picking a teacher. Beware of a teacher with too big an ego who does not exude the milk of human kindness. You are you and you have to decide what kind of teacher will serve you best. There is no simple way to find a good teacher who is right for you. Competence and character are the key criteria. It is also helpful if the teacher has a comprehensive approach to learning style by understanding the social, political, and historical context of the pieces. Background perspective helps produce correct performance.

As for me, I learn best in a relaxed, open atmosphere where the teacher is friendly and happy and not too demanding. How would you have liked to work as the organist under J.S. Bach? It is hard to imagine a more difficult gig. Or, how would you have liked to have Ty Cobb as your batting instructor? How about cooking on a routine daily basis for Julia Child? These people have achieved such great things in their field that a student is unlikely to measure up to their standards. So, it's a no-win situation. With teachers of that ilk, you will never be fully successful.

A Music Book Without Dogma

A music book that is not embarrassed but actually embraces controversy. That's good. And controversy, rational debate, and reasoned dialogue, are good for this book and good for you because this book is an attempt to help you, the individual student, find out for yourself the best path to your best and most fulfilling music education: there being no single best path to that goal, just as there is no single best path to the truth. The compulsion to think that there is only one correct path to proper musical achievement reveals an irrationally idealized approach to a gigantically complex subject. Simple solutions to complex problems never work (because if they did work then the problem, by definition, could not have been complex). General algorithms can be used for run-of-the-mill things, but they quickly fall apart when the music needs discerning and passionate performance by an individual artist.

One thing stands clear: This book and its discussion of the general issues of music memory, performance, and technique will prove useful to those who are lovers of the piano, even adult lovers of the piano, even some adult lovers of the piano as old as the hills as myself. If this book has any value, it is because it is authentic—the real deal, real experiences by a real amateur.

Attention Readers! Here comes Doctor Patten's advice on how to read this book

The usual author in the usual book doesn't dictate to his readers how the book should be read. This is not the usual book, nor is the author the usual author. Accordingly, be warned: this is not a book for the lazy or for the faint-hearted. It is not an arm-chair exemplar of easy reading. Au contraire! It is a book for study and diligent labor with a piano, pen, music sheets, and, above all, a thinking cap close at hand.

There are exercises and suggestions for the reader to invent his/her own exercises. If you feel you can't or won't do the work by concentrating your full attention for some time each day, say one hour (what's one hour to a diligent student or hobbyist?), then gently place this book back on the shelf where you found it. It's not for you. Go watch TV.

Part One

"For use can change the stamp of nature."—Aristotle
The above statement is misquoted by Shakespeare as "For use can often change the stamp of nature."

You can change your brain. Yes, you can. You change your brain by using it.

Recent research shows that mental exercise is as beneficial to the brain as physical exercise is to the muscles and that the mental exercise of playing a musical instrument decreases the chance of developing dementia and has the ability to reverse the minimal cognitive impairment that usually occurs as people get older.

Most of that recent evidence comes from neuroscience, the science of the brain and nervous system. In fact, the overwhelming neuroscientific evidence shows that directed mental activity, while decreasing the chance of Alzheimer's disease and other dementias, favorably changes the actual structure and function of the brain. Magnetic resonance scans of the brain show that just 30 minutes of piano practice will alter, rearrange, and grow neuronal (nerve cell) connections. The new rewiring will last about ten days even if there is no further practice. Scans show musical training increases brain gray matter volume and cortical networks. Musicians have better-structured corticospinal tracts. Cerebellar volumes in keyboard players actually increase with increased practice.

Some benefits of piano playing may not be scientifically demonstrable, like the mental focus and the self-discipline that years of practice engender. Nevertheless, those two benefits are there as well as the satisfaction of being part of a musical group and the feelings of self-confidence that come from having performed pieces many times before large and small groups. These intangibles count even though they can't be measured on a standardized test or the magnetic scans.

Consider this: We know the right hand is mainly controlled by the left hemisphere of the brain. The left hand is mainly controlled by the right hemisphere of the brain. Playing the violin requires both hands. But which hand does most of the complicated work? The left hand. The fingers of the left hand manipulate the strings. The right hand just works the bow. So, in violinists, we would predict that the right hemisphere motor cortex expands and may actually take over neighboring regions ordinarily devoted to the palm. And that is exactly what the scans show.

Specialization counts. Brains are tuned or actually tune themselves to the instrument played. If you play the flute, your brain will encode the sounds of the flute more richly than will the brain of a nonflautist. A pianist will recognize right away if a piano is out of tune, whereas a nonpianist might not actually hear a difference.

The results of mountains of psychological testing prove that playing the piano and other similar directed mental effort leads to better memory, improved clarity of thought, and superior powers of concentration, expression, and personal presentation. Besides which, playing the piano can be a thing of great beauty and also a thing of great fun.

The Large Structure of This Book

The content of this book divides itself like ancient Gaul into three parts across two volumes.

Part I (this part) discusses the general properties of the human brain with particular attention to those things like memory which are so essential to good piano performance.

Part II covers materials and methods—the means and general items that relate to what you need to develop good performance and the general equipment you may need for your piano playing.

A follow-up volume will illustrate the application of Parts I and II to the memorization of piano pieces for performance in recital and at festivals and for the purpose of winning contests and trophies, and for the individual egotistical purpose of showing off—showing off at home, at work, at school, at parties, and at any other suitable place or venue. Showing off includes showing off for yourself. The recognition of your personal progress in playing the piano will be gratifying and will increase as you continue your piano hobby.

Parts I and II are basically easy reading. The follow-up volume is real work and not for sissies. My guess is few readers will have the power or interest in getting through the next volume, but those who do will be richly rewarded.

My Hope

As mentioned, I hope that experience as student will provide food for thought and action to three great groups of amateur piano players:

1. Kids forced to play the piano by their parents.
2. Kids who enjoy playing the piano.
3. Adults of three types: Adults who did piano in their youth, gave it up, and now want to go back. Adults who currently are playing the piano as a hobby and who want to improve and adults who never played but want to play the piano as a hobby for entertainment and fun.

WHAT THIS BOOK DOES NOT COVER

❖ ❖ ❖

Not Covered: Improvisation

Improving your improvisation is a gigantic topic and much neglected in current music pedagogy. Many books could be written on the subject and should be written. But not by me—not yet. Improv is an ongoing process, a new style that takes time to learn. Instead of beating up on yourself that you can't do it, you have to practice improv to get better at improv. You have to kick your piano ego and take baby steps toward improvement, because your improv, at least at the beginning, will likely be much worse than your sight-reading or playing from memory.

You might even get a teacher who specializes in improv (there are such teachers) to show you the ropes. A good improv teacher will take you out of your comfort zone, develop improv tricks, expand your repertoire, and teach you to relish your freedom.

Groove and Theme

You will have to learn the basic improv moves and figures, just as you had to learn some scales. You have to learn how to find the groove and then fit into the groove. With improv, you experiment to improve, you learn to relax when put on the spot (it's not brain surgery), you learn to go with the flow, and, in the process, you learn to have fun and you may even discover some nice things about yourself.

Beat

Why not try some improv right now? Sit at the piano and hit middle G, then F, then E, then E again, then F, then D, D again, E again, and then C. Thus, you have made a melody from a descending fourth. Try replaying staccato or with a varied rhythm and spacing between the notes. Vary the order of the notes. Invent a beat. See how improv can be fun. Try adding some chords with the left hand. Say C major with G and F major with F.

Try the same with a descending hexachord. Start with A and work down some way. For instance, hit A, then F, then G, then E, then F, and D to middle C. Play with these notes, rearranging them to suit your taste. Look at your musical ideas from different perspectives. Relax! Smile! Have some fun!

Also Not Covered: Composition

Musical creativity should be a natural outgrowth of musical endeavors, for music is a creative art. You don't see students of oil painting slavishly copying Picassos or Renoirs. They do copy the masters of course, but not that much. The rest of the time, they are creating their own art: they are making their own statements. Why can't music students do the same? Face it: Most modern students of music are merely copying the masters who have composed before them. Most modern students of music are not innovators. They are harmless drudges who are content with playing the timeless classics. And that is peachy. If that is what you want to do, then do it.

Also Not Covered: Imaging as a Memory Tool

Our ancestors made mental images at will and projected them externally and manipulated them to suit their convenience and to help their memory. They did not have computers or much paper, so they memorized things by means of visual images which they constructed in their mind's eye. From 400 to 1200 AD, creative thinking and memory mostly involved the manipulation of visual images and not the use of words. The evidence for this is massive and may be found in Mary Carruthers' *The Craft of Thought*.

For instance, to remember the three parts of prudence, our ancestors made a mental picture of a wolf, lion, and dog (symbols of past, present, and future) below three human faces. The old man at the left of the image symbolized the past, the man in the middle symbolized the present, and the younger man on the right symbolized the future. The old man recalls the past memory and experience, the man in the middle intelligence, and the young man at the right provision for the future. Therefore, the three parts of prudence were memoria, intelligentia, and providentia. See the picture by Titian.

Images were also used as memory aids not only to teach religious ideas and ethics but also to aid in practical situations. For instance, consider the example given in the *Rhetorica ad Herennium*, of the imagining of the scene of a sick man in his bedroom, to whom a physician, carrying a ram's testicles on his fourth finger, offers a cup. That image is intended to recall the chief issues of a case at law. This image was not to enable a word-for-word recitation of a memorized speech but was used as a readily constructible narrative of related points, each of which cues a particular subject in the case. The image will help an attorney compose his speeches ex tempore, in response to the actual flow of the court proceedings. Can you guess the number of witnesses involved in this case? This is a play on words: Testes in Latin means witnesses and therefore there are four in this case because the testicles are on finger four. Silly, right? But effective for memory.

Not Covered—Mental Images

In my view, modern humans are fully capable of making mental images just as our ancestors did. I firmly believe we have the ability to project images into the external space just like the saints and just like the heroes of the *Aeneid*. This ability is suppressed by our current educational institutions and in general discouraged by our society. I think visual images are suppressed because the projected vivid visual images too closely resemble hallucinations and therefore might suggest mental illness.

When I taught patients at the memory clinic at Columbia University how to make mental images, I usually started with a coke bottle and had the patient make an image which they then could project onto a white wall. Some patients were then able to manipulate the image by making the coke bottle bigger or smaller and some could change the color of the bottle and invert it. The side effect of such treatment was that the coke bottle often reappeared just as the patient was about to go to sleep. This phenomenon is known in psychological circles as a hypnagogic hallucination. It is harmless and a normal phenomenon.

In fact, just before going to sleep is a good time to develop imaging skills. Just before I dose off, I can see with my eyes closed the current score that I am working on and actually read the notes from the mental image. You can do the same if you work on it. Also, you can train yourself to make projected mental images of people. Study a picture of someone just before you go to bed. Then try to make a mental image of that person with your eyes closed. At first, you will see only a vague oval outline of the face, but after a few nights of work, you may be able to actually see the whole face in vivid detail. Skeptical? Don't believe this is possible? Let me cite a historical example:

Vivid mental imaging was a fundamental component of the edifice of discipline and religious training that the converted Spanish soldier Ignatius of Loyola developed for the members of the Society of Jesus, which he founded in 1540. He had been marshalling his arguments in writing in the early drafts of his spiritual exercises, which were published eight years later. The basic idea was that his followers might vividly experience (in his words "might live") the biblical narrative in all its force. Ignatius instructed them to make in their minds mental images of Jerusalem and to follow in their mind's eyes the path which Christ traveled toward his passion. His was the first clear discussion of the use of multiple modalities to experience Jesus in a vivid personal way. Ignatius tells his people to smell the indescribable fragrance and taste the boundless sweetness of divinity, to touch by kissing and clinging, listen to the holy breath, and to use vision to fix the memory. In other words, Ignatius uses all five senses not just the visual modality in order to deepen the experience of union with Jesus himself. No wonder some of the saints to follow him had visual and personal experiences of the Blessed Mother and other biblical people actually appearing to them in the solitude of their rooms. These saints were not crazy. They were merely experiencing the natural extrapolation of the spiritual exercises, projecting to an external world that which always existed in the internal world of their minds.

Albert Einstein—Visually Mediated Thinking

Einstein as a child had great difficulty with words. He didn't speak until the age of three. His early speech was described as a laborious searching. Each spoken sentence, no matter how commonplace, was repeated silently with his lips, a practice he was finally able to abandon (according to his uncle Winteler-Einstein) at age seven.

Even in adult life, Einstein's verbal disabilities persisted. He once remarked to R.S. Shankland, "When I read, I hear the words. Writing is difficult, and I communicate this way very badly." (Einstein 1963). His non-verbal abilities, however, provided a sharp contrast. He had remarkable abilities to manipulate visual images which he constructed in his own mind. These mental images are the foundations of general and special relativity theory, the mathematical basis of your GPS system, and absolutely essential for planning space flight.

History: Einstein was a very poor student in the Munich standard verbal-oriented school he had attended. He failed the language exam needed to graduate, so his parents transferred him to an experimental school in Switzerland, founded by Pestalozzi, an educational reformer, who published in 1801 his ideas on visual methods of learning and teaching. Basic to Pestalozzi's approach was the view that "conceptual thinking is built on visual understanding; visual understanding is the basis of all knowledge."

That school freely used maps, diagrams, and other visual materials for instruction and encouraged making imaginative mental images. The atmosphere was relaxed and informal. Memorization in words was discouraged in favor of individual creative thinking in images. Each item of learning was carefully linked to a base image in accordance with Pestalozzi's principles.

In this situation, Einstein flourished and rose to the top of his class because he was allowed to use styles of thinking that were so congenial to himself. With the recent publication of the Einstein papers, the evidence that this style of thinking was nonverbal and visually mediated cannot be doubted.

The psychologist, Max Wertheimer, a friend of Einstein, had many opportunities to question the physicist on the concrete events in his thinking process that led to Einstein's theory of relativity. Einstein told him: "Thoughts did not come in any verbal formulation. I very rarely think in words at all. A thought comes, and I may try to express it in words afterwards." (Wertheimer 1945).

Responding to Jacques Hadamard (1945) Einstein provided an insight into his thought process:

"For me, it is not dubious that our thinking goes on for the most part without the use of words."

What's the Point?

In the practice of neurology, when we have a patient with a disability, we look for a compensating skill and try to develop that. In the case of Albert Einstein, we see a disability in the verbal realm overcome by skill in the visual realm.

Memory and thought are extremely complex and dependent on modality, duration, and brain function. By using unusual modalities and specific visual strategies for remembering and for problem solving, it is possible to achieve great success. Keep this in mind. Try to develop your non-verbal skills. The total thinking power of the average person can be expanded by proper application and study of the lost art of imaging. Probably maps, diagrams, and pictures of a musical score will help those of us who can form mental images. Such skills need to be better understood and taught by those in the know. The nearest thing that comes close to using visual methods to master a musical piece is Sally Christian's videos on YouTube. She constructs maps, diagrams, and pictures, with parts of pieces often displayed in different colors to help you master the structure of the classical masterpieces. Her map of *Fur Elise* was downloaded by me and helped me understand the structural organization of *Fur Elise*. Sally's map helped me master the piece.

My personal problem with visualization is that I can make a mental image of the score and read the notes from the image. But the process takes too long to be useful in performance. So, I must rely on other memory tricks to get things straight. For me, narration, mnemonics, intellectual analysis, repetition, and landmarks are effective, and I will explain how I apply them later. Meanwhile, those of you who are skilled at using visual images for your memory work should continue to exercise and develop your skill. More power to you! If you want to know more about how to develop your own imaging abilities, take a look at *Put Your Mother on the Ceiling* by Richard de Mille (Viking Compass 1973, as listed in the bibliography). When you finish that book, you will be able to put a visual image of your mother on the ceiling.

Some Ideas to Consider

Let's see more music of the 21st century—new sounds, multitonalities, mixed meters, aleatoric (chance) composition, creative pedal effects, tone clusters, ametric music (like Eric Satie's), and so forth, not to mention whole tone and pentatonic scales. Let's see the creative and innovative spirit of modern art applied to music. But don't go too far and don't hurt your piano in an attempt to get some unusual sounds the way John Cage does, stuffing his instrument with bolts, screws, rubber erasers, and other junk (the so-called prepared piano).

Music is a creative art and that means composition should be part of your fun. Why not spend ten minutes each day just experimenting and trying to develop your own pieces? For starters, hit only the black notes and devise a pattern melody that suits your fancy. The piece will sound interesting and oriental. You can even, with a little work and practice, play such a piece for the entertainment of friends and family. Try it!

Music ought to awaken the creative voice in us, in our hearts, in our minds, and in our souls, and that, friends, means composition. Bach wanted us to make our own inventions. So why not? There is an artificial division in modern conservatories and colleges between performance and creation, a division between performance and composition that should not exist. In the past, it was unthinkable to separate composition from performance. Think of Beethoven, Mozart, Prokofiev, and Rachmaninoff.

Music, then Music Memory

Keep in mind, first and above all is the music—then comes music memory. Your first duty is to be musical. We will give you some ideas and techniques on how to improve your performance and your music memory in a reasonable amount of time and with fewer tears, but you are the person who will create the music. In the next volume, we may even learn how to memorize a piece by Mozart the way I did. Then again, we may not learn a Mozart piece. I may prefer to work on Chopin. The future is contingent. Let's see.

The Mozart Effect

Just mentioning Mozart reminds me of the Mozart Effect. And that is an excellent example of how our minds work. One item tends to recall the other if that item has been previously associated in the consciousness. So, when I thought of Mozart, my mind also thought of—was channeled into thinking about—the Mozart Effect. Two items (Mozart and Mozart Effect) once connected in the consciousness, each tends to recall the other and usually more strongly in the order that they were originally connected.

Memory Facts

All memory is helped by association. Once two items are associated in the consciousness, each tends to recall the other and usually in the order presented. For example, I say the letter A. What do you think of? Usually, A recalls B as that is the way we learned the alphabet. A was associated with B in the conscious mind in the order A followed by B and thus A recalls B.

If you can associate a new item to be remembered with something you already know, your ability to recall the new item will be greatly enhanced. Any association will trigger memory and that includes smell, taste, sounds, vision, and touch. Proust was able to write a seven-volume novel by starting with a taste association from a cookie (the famous episode of the madeleine) that recalled to him his youthful days. Our ancient ancestors, particularly those of the Middle Ages like Saint Thomas Aquinas or Albertus Magnus, memorized images in places and then attached the new items to be remembered to the previously memorized place images.

Many modern mnemonists, like Harry Loraine or Bruno Furst, have prearranged peg lists to which they attach the new items to be recalled. For instance, who was the thirteenth President of the United States? You don't know. Don't feel bad. Most people don't know and actually don't care. But Harry Loraine has a peg list of images from one to 300. His image for number 13 is a tomb because, to him, $1 = T$ and $3 = m$ (mentally he rotates the 3 counterclockwise so that it looks like, that is reminds him of, an m). And the sound of tm suggests (actually reminds him of) the word tomb which then brings forth in his mind a picture of a tomb. Harry sees in his mind's eye himself driving up to a gas station in a tomb. It sounds absurd because it is absurd, but the human brain pays careful attention to the unusual, the bizarre, the violent, and the absurd. Harry tells the boy to "fill her up" and that reminds him of Fillmore. The whole recall process occurs with the speed of thought and the answer pops into the conscious mind immediately without much effort. With the peg list as the memory frame, Harry can name all the presidents of the United States in or out of order. As I have completed the Harry Loraine course in memory isometrics, I can do the same. You could also if you wished to train yourself to think that way. By the way, Harry proved to me that he memorized the Manhattan telephone book. Yes, a trained human memory is that good. Soon we'll talk about the memory competitions so you can get an idea of your own memory potential. Neurologists know there is no essential limit to human memory. Neurologists know most people have excellent memories. Human memory played a major role in the evolutionary survival of our species. Our ancestors had to remember where the berries were, what snakes to avoid, how to hunt the buffalo, and so forth. Memory was a major survival tool way back when. Still is.

A Classical Example of the Application of a Memory Tool

Cicero delivered all of his speeches in the Roman Senate from memory. He discusses his memory methods in his book *Ciceronis Rhetorica De Oratore*. He used his villa as a memory frame. He would visit individual pictures or frescos and then associate that location with a specific item he wished to remember as part of his speech. The point here is to associate the item to be remembered with a specific image in a specific place as a memory hook or peg to facilitate recall. The other important point about memory is to divide and conquer. Cicero made no attempt to memorize his speech all at once. He had to divide it into pieces that he could chunk into his memory. A normal human can only commit to memory small chunks at a time—psychologists say five to seven items max unless a large pattern is recognized. Of course, Cicero would then mentally go through his villa, look at the places he used as memory hooks, and recall the deposited items. Review and rehearsal were the keys to perfect or near-perfect recall and performance.

Divide and Conquer

Break up your memory task into bite-sized pieces that are easy to assimilate. Then link the pieces together. Do not rely on your natural memory. It is too frail. Always prop up your natural memory with the memory tricks.

For instance, if you want to remember a poem and be able to recite it verbatim, start with small phrases and don't try to memorize the whole thing at once. With music, this advice might actually reduce to working measure by measure and sometimes even just a part of a measure. In memorizing music, especially popular songs, I found, the best frame is to memorize the lyrics and be able to recite them verbatim. Review the melody by listening to renditions on YouTube. Be able to hum or sing it yourself. Then attach the melody to the lyrics using the lyrics as the memory framework. Try it. It will greatly increase your fun and greatly facilitate your memory of the piece. Of course, as you are memorizing the piece, your mind is also focusing (often unconsciously) on other sensory input that will help the associations that bring back the memory. Among other things, these include the sounds of the notes, the position of the fingers and hands on the keyboard, the picture of the score on the page and in your head, the feel of the keys to your touch, the glare and reflection of light on the piano and page, and so forth. Try to recognize and note as many details as possible. Each detail will act as an association that may help recall. Ask yourself questions to focus your attention. What's at the top of the page? What's at the bottom? What's in the middle? How does this piece start? How does it end? What's the range of pitches? Any patterns? Repetitions? Sequences? Key? Meter? Tempo? Where is the climax of the piece?

Ask yourself questions to clarify what you are observing, focus your attention, and potentially use observed items as associations to facilitate memory and recall. Meditate on the task and plan an attack to actually memorize it. Aim if you can for an intertextual (an exegesis) understanding of the piece. Why was it written? When? By whom? For whom? Reading about the composers and about the piece itself on Wikipedia will be helpful. The more rounded out your general musical knowledge, the richer and more authentic your interpretation and experience will be. Answers to such questions might help feed your memory with more associations. The more you know about your piece, the better off you will be. The brain does not tire of associations, and the more associations you make, the easier will be the recall of specific material.

Summary of Some of the Above Memory Tips

1. Divide the task into small pieces.

2. Develop a memory framework onto which you attach the new items to be recalled. Some people use numbers, others use the alphabet, others use actual locations in their homes. Some use multiple frames depending on the task and how they feel at the time. Others construct a narration about the piece. Stories are recalled quite well, so if you can make some sort of story about your piece, you will be better off. A story is a narration of events in time. The king died and then the queen died. That's a story. What happened after the king died? Answer: The queen died. See how the story can remind you. A plot is even a better memory tool. The king died and then the queen died of a broken heart. The plot gives the reasons for events and reasons help recall. What did the queen die of? Answer: The queen died of a broken heart. I love to memorize the lyrics from *The Great American Songbook*. Then I use the lyrics as a verbal frame (and emotional frame) on which to hang the melodies and the chord structure. Try this. It may help you as much as it helps me. The lyrics make sense, so there is often an additional intellectual, philosophical, and moral association.

Yes, make associations that make sense to you to help recall the memory items. The narration and the association need not be complex. The way

I remember that part three of *Maple Leaf Rag* starts with an Ab major chord is I say part three equals Ab and I see my hands on Ab major in the right hand and two Eb's (the V) in the left. Once that gets me started, everything else flows.

If need be, make the associations vivid, unusual, bizarre, or violent to help recall. A Mozart piece I memorized starts with a Bb. In my mind's eye, I see a bee with a flat tire. A bee with a flat tire (the bee has four tires just like a car—crazy right?!) reminds me to start with that Bb note. Strangely, once you get the beginning of a piece, a chain of associations usually follows and helps get you through.

3. Repeat and review by testing yourself to make sure you actually know the piece by heart. Be patient. Enjoy the practice and enjoy memorizing. Play slowly at first if you need to. Sometimes slow practice tends to cement memory in some people.

4. Sometimes you just need the right "cue" to jog your memory. Seeing an old photo or reading an old letter, hearing a song, or smelling a particular food can all be cues to activate memories. Remembering the Mozart piece starts with Bb, for instance, triggers a chain of recall for me that helps me play the whole piece.

5. When something unexpected pops into your mind, think about what is happening and see if you can identify the environmental cue or the random thought that brought the unexpected item to consciousness. When you pay attention to the association tool of memory, you will be better equipped to understand it and to use it effectively for your memory tasks.

6. Remember when you practice at home, the associations are all at home. If you play in a different environment, then the new scene will tend to interfere with recall. Every real music student has had the experience of learning a piece by heart and being able to play it perfectly at home, only to fall apart when trying to play the same piece at the teacher's studio. How come? The reason is that the teacher's place is different. Perhaps the wallpaper is green instead of brown, or there is the teacher's cute little white dog in the room listening to the music, or perhaps the lighting is different or the home has a different smell, maybe the keys are harder or easier to press or the tones are slightly different from your piano at home and so forth. No two pianos sound the same. What we are dealing with here is what the psychologists call state-dependent learning. It's a good idea to understand state-dependent learning so that you can deal with it effectively.

State-Dependent Learning

A patient came to my memory clinic with the chief complaint, "I forgot where I hid the money." He is a parish priest who received what he considered a rather large donation ($3,000). He and a fellow priest decided to celebrate and went on what most people would call a bender. Yes, drink had been taken. When they awoke the next day, neither priest could remember much of what had happened during the celebration, nor did they know what happened to the money.

What advice would you give these priests to help them remember what happened to the money? Do you think it is possible to recover from an alcohol-induced memory blackout?

My advice was for one of the priests to get drunk again while in the company of his fellow priest, who would remain sober. Said I, "Start drinking at the same rate, the same whiskey, at the same time of day in the same room wearing the same clothes that you wore on the day the loss occurred. Duplicate as much as possible the brain state that occurred when the money and the memory were misplaced. Get into the same celebratory mood you had on the day the loss occurred. Duplicating the brain state should remind you what happened to the money."

Of course, the priests followed the advice to the letter even though two other neurologists had advised them with the then-standard wisdom that the memory was lost forever and that it was impossible to recover a memory after an alcohol-induced blackout.

Result: What happened to the money flashed into the drunk priest's mind. The priests had hidden the money in the light fixture of the priest's room. He even recalled the reason he hid the money: He didn't want his housekeeper to know about it.

Conclusion: The priest's brain hid the money under the brain state which we would call drunk. Getting that brain again under the influence helped recall. Multiple other examples of state-dependent memory will be given. This is an important topic for your music memory work. So, pay attention.

State-Dependent Learning Is Real and Really Important

Astronauts who have trained on Earth where there is gravity, learned a task, and repeated it over 100,000 times often have trouble even starting the task when they are in space where there is no gravity. The reason for this is the brains of the astronauts in space are in a different brain state than they were on Earth. When the astronauts return to Earth, they again easily recall the task they learned on Earth. The reverse is also true. A task learned in space is more easily recalled in space than on return to Earth. Brain recall is state-dependent, and the more closely the recall situation resembles the situation during learning, the better the chance of recall.

Divers who learn a task while they are underwater have trouble recalling the task while they are on land. But when back underwater, they can recall the task without apparent effort. Ditto the reverse: What's learned on land, they have trouble remembering during the dive.

What Does State-Dependent Learning Mean in Relation to Music Memory?

State-dependent learning means that for effective recall, the brain must be in the same physical state or a state that is similar or reasonably similar to the state it was in during the actual learning process. Otherwise, there may be problems.

My experience with *The Promenade* in *Pictures at an Exhibition* by Modeste Mussorgsky is a case in point. After months of work, I was able to play this piece without apparent effort, almost automatically, and did play it hundreds of times without difficulty and I made a YouTube of the piece. One day, I had serious acid indigestion. Surprise! No matter how hard I tried, I couldn't get it right. The next day, when I felt normal, there was no problem. The indigestion put my brain in a different state from the state during which I usually played this piece, and that difference was enough to foul my memory. When you are sick, forget about trying to memorize anything and concentrate on getting better.

Quiz time: What would be a better way of training memory for a piano piece: Playing individual hands separately until perfect or practicing both hands together?

Answer: Both hands together would more closely simulate playback conditions, and separate hands would not. And yet, you will find in the bibliography books written by qualified teachers who urge memorization one hand at a time. This is not my recommendation as it contradicts what I know about state-dependent learning. If you practice with separate hands, that is, in fact, what you learn, and then you have to relearn how to play the piece with hands together as is usually required during performance. However, if hands apart and then together works for you, then do your thing that way.

Anxiety and Stage Fright

Anxiety and stage fright alter brain chemistry and electrical activity, often placing the brain in a different state from the brain's state during practice. Thus, during anxiety, playback conditions differ from learning conditions. Consequently, there may be trouble. Hence, inexperienced pianists are often surprised that during recitals, they flub the piece they did so well so many times at home and in the studio.

The treatment for this varies. Experience helps calm recital and public playing fears. Good teachers teach how to avoid performance anxiety. Overlearning the task also helps. Horowitz, for instance, is known to play the same piece several hundred times so that he won't go blank during performance. We amateurs need not be so diligent. Learning under multiple conditions of brain function will also help. Repeat the piece when tired, when wired from too much coffee, when unhappy, when happy, when elated. Repeat whenever you can before whatever audience you can drum up. Repeat your piece at different times during the day and night. Try to encode the sequences at several levels of brain states and conditions. That way, you will have increased your chance of correct readout from the long-term memory no matter what the environmental conditions or situation. I play as many different pianos as I can. I used to keep a list of all the pianos I have played. Eight years ago, I stopped compiling the list at piano 183. Experienced public speakers visit the venue of their speech to check things out: What's the acoustics? The lighting? The rostrum? How many seats in the audience? In fact, experienced public speakers profit by visiting the venue in advance and actually practicing their speech there and then.

Whenever possible, I do the same, and I play the piano at the venue ahead of time because every piano sounds different, and I want my brain to understand what the performance instrument actually sounds like. I also script and rehearse the anticipated events: How to ascend the stage, how to bow, how to smile, and how to act like I am fully confident that my performance will be a hit.

Whenever possible, simulate playback conditions as close as you can get to practice conditions. (Wear the same clothes, eat the same breakfast, drink the same cup of coffee, develop the same frame of mind as you had in practice at home.) If you don't think the general atmosphere in which you memorize your piece is important, then try this experiment: Memorize a short piece completely such that you can play it without error and without hesitations. Do the memory work only at a specified time of the day—say morning time. Once you are sure you know this piece completely and play it without difficulty every morning, then test yourself by playing it at night. I think you will find there is a difference in your performance. The reason for this is the brain has associated a given time and place with the piece that you have memorized. When you change the environmental conditions, the brain gets confused, and memory suffers. The treatment for this problem is to play the piece many times under many different conditions, morning and night, so your brain gets used to different environments and adapts to them. Personal confession: I also practice my cocktail party repertoire after I have had a drink or two. That way, I am in a certain brain state prepared at dinner parties and in certain restaurants. When they ask me to play the piano, I can do so without much trouble. I usually start with *Stormy Weather*, and if that goes over OK, I advance to *The Man I Love*.

During your performance, try to stay focused. Be confident, but not too confident. My usual trouble is that I start to congratulate myself halfway through—I congratulate myself for playing so well up to that point, and that is the kiss of death that causes me to lose focus and mess up. Save your self-congratulations for when your playing is over. If you make mistakes, play wrong notes, break down, forget your piece—so what! It is not a matter of life or death. Think about where things went wrong, work on corrections at home or with your teacher, and try again. My playing is never perfect. I continue to have slips, but they are not the same as when I started recitals. So what! I notice that the majority of students playing in memorized recitals have a fair share of near-misses and faking. We should strive for perfection, but as inhabitants of the real world, we should accept imperfection. The key to getting out of a memory blank is to have an exit strategy, something we will discuss soon. I usually have landmarks ahead of the piece that I can skip to if and when I go blank. Or if you are really desperate, play cadences and see if that gets you back to where you belong.

If you make a mistake, never, ever stop playing. The audience won't recognize an error or wrong notes unless you stop. Most of the audience is thinking of something else and not paying attention to your piece or not paying much attention at all. At parties, half of them are three sheets to the wind already.

Audience Inattention

Detailed studies of Harvard Law School students have proven that at any one time, about a third of the students at a lecture are thinking of something else, that is something other than what the professor is discussing. The way this study was done is interesting. Each student got a button and instructions to press the button when they realized that they had been paying attention to their own thoughts (usually about a different subject or a personal matter) rather than the professor's lecture. On average, at any one time, a third of the law students are pressing the button because they caught themselves daydreaming. If that is what happens at Harvard Law School, what happens with the run-of-the-mill usual audience will be worse, especially during cocktail hour. Therefore, most of your audience won't notice a mistake. Even if they do notice a mistake, they won't care. They are too much involved with their own problems, of which they probably have many.

Lesson

If you make a mistake, just smile, play on, and act nonchalant. Later we will give advice about rescue points (some authors call them landmarks) that you can use to disguise mistakes and make things seem whole.

The Distributive Rule

Many detailed scientific studies have shown that distributing a memory task over time is a better way of memorizing things than trying to memorize something all at once. So, one hour a day for 30 days on *Fur Elise* will net you more solid memory and a much better performance than ten hours a day for three days.

Advice: Do not cram.

Can we speak frankly? Classical music may be dying. Few audiences are impatient to hear the next classical recital. No one is screaming for more Bach or Beethoven. Classical musicians have been fighting pop culture, and losing, for decades. That is why we have to do our best to bring back the audiences. Memorized music is more their cup of tea. Focusing on entertaining the audience will help create interest. As amateur piano players, we are doing our own private preservation project of the classical tradition and popular solo music, and we are having fun in the process.

Back to The Mozart Effect

The Mozart Effect (listening to music makes you smarter) is controversial. The idea is that listening to music, classical music in particular, makes children smarter. The myth goes back to a study of undergraduate students at University of California Irvine in 1993. When students listened to one of Mozart's piano sonatas, they did better on a subset of I.Q. tests than their peers. Subsequent study showed the effect relates to overall arousal and not specifically to Mozart's music. The same result occurred when the students listened to a Stephen King novel or music by the British band Blur. My take is that entertainment can capture attention and can therefore be good for some brains.

As I don't want to get involved in more controversy, I shall keep my mouth shut and quietly let a famous neurologist address the issue. Oliver Sacks, one of the best-known neurologists in the world, was Artist in Residence at Columbia University and is now dead. Perhaps you have heard of him. His recent book *Musicophilia* has been a bestseller. Here's what Oliver Sacks (OS) said in an interview with *Neurology Now* (NN) (January/February 2008):

NN: "Is there any therapeutic difference between playing music, singing it, or listening to it?"

OS: "I don't think there's much to be said for the so-called Mozart Effect, which has to do with casual exposure to music. But I think there's a great deal to be said for active involvement with music, whether it takes the form of music therapy in a hospital or learning an instrument and following a score."

"Active mental involvement with organization of material is the key to good performance."

Notice how the great man, Oliver Sacks, emphasizes active versus passive involvement, an important point which will come up soon and then appear again and again. The current catchword for this kind of mental involvement in what you are doing is "mindfulness." In general, playing and at the same time thinking about your piece and what you are doing (mindfulness) is better than just playing the piece, which is better than just thinking about the piece, which is worlds better than just passively listening to the piece. We will return to this important idea. Meanwhile, let's talk about the benefits of memorizing your piece. Can you think of any? Stop and make a list. Then compare your list with mine:

Stop!

Did you even try to think about the benefits of playing music from memory? If you did, pat yourself on the back. If you didn't, then you are missing the benefits of being actively involved in the learning process.

Why Perform from Memory?

Although I am too lazy to do it myself, I believe that adequate historical research would show that until the nineteenth century, when musicians played in public, they either improvised the music or read the score. In the time of Bach, Haydn, and Mozart, it would have been very unusual (some say preposterous) for musicians to perform their music in public from memory and without "the book." That musicians of that era were capable of prodigious feats of memory has been proven by the case of Mozart, who wrote down Allegri's *Miserere* at first hearing. But despite excellent memories, the teachers of that era not only discouraged memory-playing but sternly forbade it; and if a pupil allowed his eyes to stray from the printed page, he was brought back to self-consciousness by the familiar reprimand, "Look at your music."

All that changed in the Romantic period where there was a trend toward individual solo performance. In the Romantic era, pianists such as Clara Wieck Schumann (1819-1896) and Franz Liszt (1811-1886) began to play in concerts without the score. The lemmings followed their lead and the situation hasn't changed much since. Now the majority of solo pianists and violinists do not use the score when giving performances of the standard repertoire. Recitals, festivals, contests, and the like almost always require that performance be done from memory. Furthermore, no difficult passage can be mastered without, early in the operation, memorizing it or at least memorizing part of it. With lots of notes that must be played fast, sometimes the only way to get through is on memory.

Sidebar About Repertoire

Your duty is to develop your own repertoire. Make repertoire your long-term project and follow my advice: memorize every worthwhile piece you play. Yes, memorize everything that you think is worthwhile. The benefits to your piano career will be beyond description. And the more you memorize, the more associations you will be able to make and the better will be your brain for more memorization. This idea is also true in life in general: The more you know, the more you can know, and the more you will know. Knowledge feeds knowledge. Can you think of a reason that knowledge feeds knowledge?

Answer: The more you know, the more associations you can make and the more you will be able to recall by associating what you knew with what is new. If you got the right answer (association is key to acquisition of knowledge), give yourself a pat on the back and take a break to reward yourself.

Old Versus New Repertoire Pieces

One thing that struck me when I started music lessons (at age—oh, never mind) was the weird semi-official obsession with the works of dead composers. No other art worth its salt is like that. Theater, movies, dance, painting, ceramics, golf, downhill skiing, neurosurgery, and so forth stay for the most part contemporary. When theater features a play by Eugene O'Neill, one speaks of a revival. But we don't speak of a Beethoven revival. Music as an art (not as an entertainment) seems to hover over a faded past. In all the recitals that I have performed in (and suffered through), over 90 percent of the pieces played have been over a century old. In our so-called contemporary festival in Clear Lake, Texas, no contemporary American music was played, and the Bartók and Prokofiev pieces proffered as "modern" were over 50 to 70 years old. Music teachers, it is my opinion, when they think of composers tend to think of them in the grave. Help correct this situation: Put some living composers in your repertoire. Eugenie Rocherolle and Mona Rejino are among my favorites. Look kindly on the music of those more recently deceased than Beethoven: Harold Arlen, George and Ira Gershwin, Scott Joplin, to name a few. Why not loosen up and have recitals with a more modern edge? The *In Recital* series with popular music with Doctor Helen Marlais as editor is a good place to start (FJH Music Company), and the *Outside the Box* series is on the cutting edge.

Performing from Memory Is Scary

As every real student of music knows, performing from memory can be a difficult and anxiety-provoking task, especially at the beginning. So why do it? We would argue that memorization of a piece can be a fulfilling experience that alone justifies the effort and the current tradition.

The pieces that I have memorized are the pieces that I understand better, in some cases much better. There is a difference between learning a piece and being intimately familiar with it. Memory enables intimate familiarity. Those of you who have already had the privilege of memorizing some pieces know exactly what I am talking about. Those of you who have not had the privilege of memorizing a piece don't know what I am talking about, but sometime in the, I hope, not too distant future, you will be in for a great treat and a great revelation once you do manage to memorize a piece.

Memory and Repetition Go Hand in Hand with Learning and Appreciation

In the classical pieces, review, restudy, and memory help uncover some of the boundless messages, feelings, emotions, and ideas in the great music. This is the reason that great pianists never tire of pieces they have performed hundreds of times. These are artists who have played the same piece for over 50 years. Their latest recording compared to the early recordings often proves that the music has for them taken on new meanings. And we would bet that even composers never fully understand all that is embedded in their works.

My friend, Walter Hilse (a composer who has a PhD in music from Columbia University), says that what he does is present a work and hope that the performer will grow into it, find new statements every time it is played, and add part of their own personality and interest to the performance. Which reminds me (by association) of the interesting experiences that I have had listening to composers play their own compositions. Can you recall what they were? Test yourself.

WHAT HAPPENS (SOMETIMES) WHEN COMPOSERS PLAY THEIR OWN PIECES—A REVIEW OF WHAT JIMMY WHITE TAUGHT

❖ ❖ ❖

They raise their hands and often fall on the wrong notes! Mind you, these artists are not undermining themselves. They are trying to play what they heard in composing. Their music is on paper, not in the performance. Often, they have not memorized, nor do they know or have a feeling for their own creation. They have a right to play it any way they wish, of course, but lesser mortals (like ourselves) wouldn't dare to imitate them. Don't believe me? Listen to the recordings of Debussy playing his own works. Or Ravel. (Debussy played his own pieces straighter than Ravel played his, but both are often way off the scores with lots of wrong notes. Yet, the overall effect is actually good.)

When composers play the compositions of others, the effect is even more interesting and sometimes terrible. They are less maniacal than "real" music teachers and certain pianists, especially about historical truths, which are often not true and often not historical.

So what? What's the point? Only this: If the composers are making mistakes playing their own works, or if composers are not so fanatical about absolute reproduction of the musical score, then why should we ordinary mortals be so concerned about perfection? Perfection is often the enemy of the good.

Groove

Sometimes I worry that music students and music teachers take things too seriously. Once or twice this has troubled my sleep. At the recitals and festivals that I have participated in, too many students are seen struggling with anxiety, stress, and worry. What for? Is it really worth it? Aren't these kids entitled to their childhood? Fears and anxiety probably have a negative effect on performance and even on the whole process of learning; certainly, they are antithetical to the creation of true art. The pressure of perfection can be unhealthy in routine practice and learning settings. Good enough is often good enough. The more enjoyable the learning experience, the more will be learned.

In my view, I think Teacher Ying Zhang will agree: the composers, by showing their imperfections and their human face, are giving us a license to relax, lighten up, and not worry so much about the exact reproduction of the piece. The overall expression is more important than minor errors.

Lesson: Kick your perfection ego in the face and get out there and play, play in the original sense of the word (recreational amusement). In other words, with music, work less; play more and have more fun.

Practical Matters

Some of the arguments for memory devolve on practical matters. For example, memorizing music dispenses with cumbersome page turns. No page turns mean you can not only go faster, but also that you do not have to interrupt the continuity of the piece to turn the page. (That isn't always true. Some pieces have rests when you turn the page, but most do not and therefore the page turn is usually an interruption, an interruption that is unwelcome.)

With memory, lighting is no longer much of a problem.

Phrasing is better with a memorized piece.

An interpretation is more personal with a memorized piece.

When I look at a piece, I always imagine what it would be like to memorize it. Consequently, I make better repertoire choices because I had to think hard about what I decided to learn and what I decided not to learn. This, believe it or not, is an important decision. In my view, it is wrong to attempt to learn a piece you don't like.

Theme and Upbeat

With memory, (this may sound stupid) I travel lighter. When visiting friends and relatives, or when away on vacation, I am not burdened by carrying the music around with me. Unencumbered, I just sit at the piano and play some of my memorized popular pieces (like *The Man I Love* or *Stormy Weather*) or classical pieces (like *To a Wild Rose* or

Piano Concerto in A Minor), whatever pieces seem appropriate for the people there around me. People are impressed that I can just sit down and create something beautiful out of my memory and out of my head. Think about this: What is the different effect on an audience of reading a poem to them or just reciting the poem from memory?

One of my friends, Justin Sobieski, does carry his music in a big knapsack and plops it on the living room floor before he opens up to get his music to play for informal friends! This is awkward, time-consuming, and discourteous. And not without lots of fumbling to locate the piece he wants to play.

My teachers won't believe this: I think playing from memory has made me much more aware of tone issues. In fact, I can recognize the tone of a Kawai from a Yamaha, a Steinway D from a Steinway Baby Grand. I can hear the difference between a keyboard and a Sauter and an Essex upright. I can even tell the difference in tone on a Baldwin (which I play at the College of Mainland) and the Mason & Hamlin Model A Grand, that I play at the Arlington Resort Hotel & Spa, Hot Springs, Arkansas. And yes, tone awareness lets me know when a piano is out of tune and how much.

With memory, the music support panel doesn't block the sound. I have tested this fact with my video recordings for YouTube. That little support panel that you use to hold the music does block the sound coming from the piano and somehow changes the sound so that it is less mellow.

With memory, my technique is more solid. Memory work requires lots of repetition, often slow repetition at the beginning, and such repetition gives greater accuracy.

Also, every real pianist knows that certain pieces are impossible to play well without memorizing them. And (don't tell your teacher I said this), a memorized piece lets you look at the keys more.

With playing from memory, I notice fewer neck and back issues.

With memory, I feel the memorized piece is part of me, part of my spirit. A memorized piece is as spiritually helpful as the memory of a good vacation or the memory of a nice meal or the memory of the love of another person. Memories become part of us. We own them and there is a certain pride and often a pleasure in ownership.

Last but not least, is the existentialist problem of finding a meaning to one's life. Often there is no meaning. So, you have to construct a meaning. This may sound strange to those of you who are not used to philosophy, but developing a purpose and focus to your piano playing can be a part of the meaning of your life. By developing a meaning for your life, you become more of a human being with more of a sense of control of your own destiny. As for me, I have developed a large collection of solo pieces that I record and upload onto YouTube. The reports each month confirm that people are listening to my work and I believe they are enjoying it as much as I enjoyed recording the pieces. Each week I work on a piece to memorize and upload. Sometimes I recite the lyrics of the great American song and then play it. The fans have praised that approach and the feedback has been gratifying. You could do the same if you wish. All of us are better off if we have purposes in living. But realistically speaking, who can decide what meanings you have in your life? Only you, you, you.

Esthetics

Other arguments devolve on esthetics. For example, memory enables musicians to focus on specific musical and communicative advantages such as freer expression and better ability to communicate their own ideas to audiences, even rubato. The player who is dependent on his notes may find reading notes not only limiting but actually an interference in achieving full artistic expression.

In any case, I believe, one must know the piece if one is to give it the right shape in performance. Knowing the piece by heart certainly helps. My take on artistic expression is that performance is an individual art form that needs human expression to achieve art's redemptive quality. A player piano, computer, street organ, or other such machine can perform but not that well, and not with feeling. Exact reproduction of a score will often result in an affectively flat, emotionless experience, whereas playing music from your deep heart's core will often produce a much-to-be-desired affectively moving, emotion-filled experience. Ugh! Sad to say most modern recital contests I have attended are about power and speed when they should be about beauty and truth.

Consider this: Which would you rather hear: a lecture where the lecturer reads the text exactly or a lecture where the lecturer actually speaks to you directly? A lecturer who looks at you, who has open body posture, who smiles, who delivers his message in human terms (by which I mean NOT PERFECT) is a better lecturer than one who reads from a paper. Perfection is the enemy of the good. By reading the paper, the message is perfect because it is directly transmitted into sound, but as a human event, it is flat and emotionless and disrespectful of the audience. Furthermore, having a paper in front of the face as one reads from a sheet detracts from the closeness of contact desired by most humans and is off-putting. Like it or not, eye contact is an important way we humans connect with each other.

My take on recent festivals and recital contests is that judges are bored stiff with the technically correct, but essentially soulless repetition of some classical pieces that they (the judges) have heard over and over again. They want life! Give it to them! My general rule is to find the mood of the piece and play it so that mood is communicated to the audience. Baroque music usually has one mood per piece; classical has contrasting moods so I try to play up the contrasts. Your understanding of the mood of a piece is fundamental to your ability to interpret the piece correctly and to play musically. While on my soapbox, I may as well say that in my opinion the finest kind of interpretation is that which suggests improvisation—spontaneity, inspiration, rapid yet logical invention. Such an effect is difficult to achieve by a pianist who is playing from copy. The reason for this failing is not clear but it may relate to the fact that the audience itself is faced by the fact that the music does not proceed from the player but from some external source that the player is reading. Printed music and the page turns get between the listener and the interpretation. At best, the sheet music and the page turn are an annoyance. At worst, they may destroy the interpretation and part of the mystery of immediate creation right there in front of the audience.

Whoa! You may reply that the orchestra always plays from the printed copy. They must do this for a reason. What is the reason? I guess to stay together.

They do, but their playing would be much more impressive if they did not play from copy. The truth is that music is so intangible, so ethereal and, indeed, so mysterious that the visual introduction of the material things necessary to produce it lessens its effect. All orchestras and their conductors should be hidden from the audience. Wagner knew this when he planned his theater at Bayreuth so that the orchestra should be invisible when playing his music dramas. Some of us have often wished that the singers might be made invisible also, but that is another story.

Musical Notation is Needed for Effective Memorization

Many scholars (such as Mary Carruthers, Frances Yates, Jan M. Ziolkowski cf. bibliography) have pointed out that the era of memorization of music started when written notation started, probably for good reason: A noted score, as stated before, is your best tool in memorizing. So, I am not in any way bad-mouthing the written score. No way. We are just talking about where its place should be during performance—namely off stage and out of sight.

Brief Summary of the History of Musical Notation

Music notation is a division of semasiography, a form of writing sounds that has become the open gate to power and refinement of thought and creative expression. The musical score bypasses the use of words to express ideas, thoughts, and feelings.

Guido d'Arezzo, an Italian Benedictine monk of the eleventh century (AD 995-1050), invented the four-line staff, which he used in combination with a notation earlier developed in the eastern Roman Empire for the recitation of Christian scriptures by means of marks called neumes (from the Greek pneuma, "breath"). The neumes, similar to the markings in the Koran to assist oral recitation, were written over the text and later used to notate Gregorian chant.

Written scores are therefore none other than mnemonic devices (that is, memory aids) to remind what notes are to be sounded and how and when. The Greek system of notation with different pitches indicated by letters of the alphabet is similar and has found better application to modern music. In the fourteenth century, the staff was increased to our current familiar five lines.

Early forms of notation did not permit the recreation of the rhythm, pitch, and inflection of a composer but were identifying association-based mnemonic devices that only reminded the singer of a song whose rhythm, melody, and intonation he/she had heard and learned aurally. Listen to the YouTube versions of *Tantum Ergo* and see how each group has a different way of singing the chant. The version I sing is very different from the four on YouTube and probably reflects what I heard our parish priests sing during their version of benediction.

The further refinement of these earlier mnemonic devices (a clef that defines the ranges of pitches and shapes of notes that determine the duration of the pitch, plus other marks about intonation and phrasing) soon made previously unimaginable forms of music possible and opened the door to thinking about the inner laws of musical expression, which in turn became the technological foundation of academic musicology.

Guido's achievement, the net result of which was to make sounds visible, also made possible modern "classical music" and the modern notion of and respect for "the composer."

Here's What to Avoid

Recently, I heard a trained soprano singing a beautiful rendition of *Hark! The Herald Angels Sing,* only she was so nervous about missing something she had to glance down at the sheet and twice even turned the page. There is no excuse for such discourtesy to the audience. Her performance was the less for it.

Major Point

When words or music are out of sight, both audience and performer are free to listen more attentively and the singer is able to style the song more effectively.

If you don't think song styling is important, listen to several versions of *Blues in the Night.* Compare the style of Julie London with that of Peggy Lee. Lee's version is shorter and in jazz long short rhythm. Lee has omitted the part B verse poem and the coda (My mama was right/ my mama was right/ there's blues in the night), parts of the work that make this a classic American Art Song. Lee deemphasizes the long vowel sounds (cf. Julie London's singing of the words "done," "blow," and "blues"). It's like American Idol: same songs, different styling.

Our point about Lee and London is that both these singers have sung the same song, but each has a version that reflects her individual artistic vision. Each has created her own masterful rendition which is instantly identifiable by the song styling as hers and as the work of an individual artist. Dinah Shore has two different versions of her *Blues in the Night* proving that the same artist can have two different visions of the same song, each with unique effects. Ethel Waters and Lena Horne have two different versions of *Stormy Weather,* each adding to the legend of this classic song and each recording inducted into the Grammy Hall of Fame.

Music from Memory is Here to Stay

Face it! People not only prefer performance from memory, most modern audiences in formal settings demand it. Music from memory will not go out of fashion any more than wearing some kind of shoe will go out of fashion. Wearing shoes will be around for a long, long time—centuries because our feet need shoes. Playing from memory will be around for a long, long time—centuries because our audiences want and need it.

Other Reasons for Memorizing Are Compelling

Brainpower is augmented by memorizing. Brain scan data shows that memorizing music increases brain power enormously. Reading and playing from the score increases brain power too, but not as much.

What You Should Gain by Working Through This Book

The proper application of the principles involved here should make you perform at least twice as well as you do now. To say that you can double your performance is in point of fact an understatement. Many people will actually improve ten-fold—1000%. But notice: The claim is that you will perform better and faster. As soon as you stop using these techniques and as soon as you stop following these principles, your performance level will degrade back toward where it was. The (sad and unfortunate) reason for this is that no technique can increase your mental horsepower.

Not Yet

Doubling your mental horsepower (that is doubling your I.Q.)—That's a different problem—a horse of a different color. In the opinion of most scientists, doubling mental horsepower, doubling your I.Q., is not possible under the present state of our knowledge. Scientists don't seem to know why this is true, but it is.

But look smarter—twice as smart and perform twice as well: you bet. That's not only possible; it is probable

The Evidence That You Can Improve and Improve a Lot

Detailed psychological tests on normal people have proven that the techniques discussed here, if applied with due diligence, will objectively improve performance by at least an order of magnitude, that is, not two-fold, not three-fold, but ten-fold. Yes, a ten-fold improvement. That is what is meant by an order of magnitude. If the objective tests show ten-fold improvements, then the claim of a two-fold improvement has to be understated, modest, and fully obtainable.

Ten-Fold Improvement? What Does a Ten-Fold Improvement Actually Mean?

In other words, if it takes you ten minutes at the present time using your native basic memory to memorize five presidents of the United States, using the memory systems about to be discussed will enable you to memorize 50 presidents in the same amount of time. That is a fact, just as much of a fact as five times ten is 50.

Will the Principles and Techniques Contained Herein Become Dated and Outmoded?

No! These principles are immortal. They will not become dated or outmoded. The human brain evolved over millions of years. It is what it is and is unlikely to change in your lifetime, the lifetime of your children or your grandchildren. In fact, I would wager that the human brain will remain fundamentally the same for thousands of years and will be the same when our sun, four billion years from now, becomes a red giant and burns out our planet. Before that happens, humans will have left Earth to pollute some other world. When they leave, they will likely take their music with them, in their heads, in their hearts, and on the sheets.

Work Is Necessary

But don't get the wrong idea. This book is not written for the lazy. Some have to work hard to memorize music, some have to work a little. But all, regardless of the methods used to memorize music, must work.

A Word About General Mental Health for Pianists

If mental exercises are good for the brain, the big question is what exercises are best and what exercises are best for what purpose. The short answer to that question is that almost anything will do for anything that you actively engage your brain in doing is going to have some beneficial effect and that beneficial effect will spill over into anything else that you do. So, fill your mind with good books, interesting movies, great exhibitions, and informative lectures, even sermons. Join new groups, talk with new people, and don't be afraid of trying new things. Remake yourself into a better person.

What General Activities Benefit the Brain the Most? The Short Answer:

In general, as mentioned, the brain benefits best from active thinking and doing (the state of mind known in modern psychology as "mindfulness"), second best from doing, third best from thinking, and least from just watching and not thinking or doing.

Just watching and not doing or not thinking is just about the worst thing you can do for your brain's health and happiness.

That's why so many neurologists (myself included) hate TV (yes, hate is the right word). For TV is just junk food for the mind—empty content without intellectual value in the same way that junk food is empty calories without nutritional value. James J. Gibson in his pioneering studies of military pilot training discovered that student pilots gain nothing from reading about piloting or from watching someone fly a plane. They get nothing much from listening to a lecture on the subject and only a little more from looking at pictures and diagrams. In fact, the thing that was most effective in training pilots was (you guessed it) having student pilots actually confront real piloting situations in the air or in a simulator. And that is why pilots train that way to this very day.

Stop and think. Does the lesson about student pilots have anything to do with learning how to play the piano?

Question: What is the best way to learn how to play the piano? Pick the correct answer from the list.

1. Watch someone play the piano.

2. Read about playing the piano.

3. Listen to a lecture about playing the piano.

4. Take lessons in which you actually play the piano.

Exercises: No Scientific Basis

As for Hannon and his famous exercises: There is no scientifically acceptable evidence that playing the exercises does anything much of benefit. Acquiring techniques is mostly a process of brain/nerve development, not finger strength. No pianist plays mainly with his or her hands, anymore than a surgeon mainly operates with his hands. It is mainly the brain that is playing, just as it is mainly the brain that is operating. Playing Hannon, like watching TV, also incurs an opportunity cost and loss. You could have been learning a great piece of music in the five to 15 minutes a day that most students spend on Hannon. And you could be learning a great piece of music in the three plus hours a day that most Americans (I kid you not) spend watching TV.

How Much TV Do Kids Watch?

Nielsen Company says in a study released October 26, 2009 that children ages two to five watch more than 32 hours of television each week (Wall Street Journal, October 27, 2009, page A4). Kids six to 11 spend a little less time in front of the TV screen—more than 28 hours. But that is partly because they have to go to school. TV isn't called the electronic babysitter for nothing. Think of all those young brains that are not getting the exercise that they need for proper development. Think about all those young muscles that are not getting the exercise they need for proper development. Think of all that wasted life!

But What About Czerny?

We are searching for ways to warm, not chill our music-making. Playing actual musical pieces is indubitably the major most important gratifying goal of amateur playing. Therefore, concentrate on pieces and not on exercises.

The best explanation I ever heard of why Czerny wrote his millions of dry notes was that which Anton Rubinstein told Egon Petri: "Czerny hated little children."

Educational TV Is Not All That Educational

But what about educational programs on PBS and TV programs of that ilk?

Next time you watch such programs, pay attention to two things: The information density and the content. You may find that the information density is slight and that the content does little more than entertain you by flattering your ego by showing you stuff you already know.

One producer from Disney (Mr. Lesiter) explained this to me directly: "The public will not tolerate anyone showing them stuff they are not already familiar with. The public wants affirmation that they already know all that they need to know. Try to teach them something new and your chance of staying in business is close to zero."

Opportunity Costs: Lost Opportunities Are Opportunities Lost

The other problem with TV is that the time spent watching it could have been better spent thinking or reading or learning or playing a musical instrument or playing chess or bingo, social dancing or doing any one of a number of activities. Any one or any combination of those activities has been shown by neuroscientists in prospective, controlled, blinded, long-term scientific studies (financed at great cost by the government) to augment brain power and reduce the chance of dementia.

Watching TV on the other hand has been shown (I am not making this up) to increase your chance of developing heart disease, diabetes, cancer (cancer of the colon in particular), obesity, and dementia. TV has been shown to seriously degrade attention span and memory capacity. Significant evidence indicates that watching TV causes autism in some cases and that stopping TV stops the autism in those cases. If it seems like I am making watching TV sound really bad, it is because watching TV is really bad.

Doctors Are Against TV

And so the austere, usually laconic, and rarely committed New England Journal of Medicine came out in an editorial against TV as detrimental to the brain. If doctors don't know what's good for the brain and what isn't good for the brain, who does?

What Activities Are Best for Your Brain? The Long Answer:

The long answer to the question about which exercises are best to help the brain memorize and perform musical pieces is this project and the advice, exercises, expositions, demonstrations, and techniques contained here in this book. Such exercises, expositions, demonstrations, and techniques evolved from medical research and experience with patients that has spanned over four decades and they have also evolved from Doctor Ying Zhang's experience with music students and music performance over decades as well. The things suggested should help you help your brain. They should, in fact, help a lot.

Positive Mental Attitude is a Positive

Studies have repeatedly shown that if you think that you can memorize a piece, if you think you can learn the piece, if you think you can perform the piece, then the probability that you will goes way up. Conversely, if you think you can't memorize a piece, if you think you can't learn the piece, if you think you can't perform the piece, then the chance of your mastering that piece is far less, probably close to zero. Doctor Patten summarizes this idea in a little poem:

If you think you can, you can
If you think you can't, you're right again
For whatever you think you can or can't
That's what you can or can't

Hint

You will have an easier time memorizing a piece if you have previously played it from notes and have felt that you have done a good job playing it. Picking up a new piece that you have not had experience with will take longer to memorize and require more work.

Failures Now Do Not Mean Failures Always

Let's say you have two or three times failed to recollect a particular passage of music. Do not assume and do not imagine that you will forget it on the next occasion that you play. A pianist who says to himself: "I know perfectly well that I shall break down in the usual place; it's no use, I simply can't remember it" is doomed to forget for this form of auto-suggestion is likely to be fatal. To imagine that you can't do a thing is to very often render oneself incapable of doing it. Moreover, it is of no service to a pianist (or to anyone else) to will himself to remember something he has assured himself that he cannot remember. Thus, when the imagination is in conflict with the will, the imagination will usually win. I am not saying the will doesn't exist, or that it is totally disabled. I am saying that under these self-imposed restrictions, the will to remember will function feebly or arbitrarily or not at all. There is a long and complicated factual explanation for this failing, but let us illustrate it in action:

Any normal person can without much difficulty walk along a twelve-inch wide plank placed on the ground. No particular balancing powers are required for such a feat. But if the same plank were projected over the edge of a cliff, not one person in 20 could walk it. Why? In the last case, the person fearing that he may fall imagines that he will do so—tells himself that he will and then believes what his imagination has told him. From that moment, his actual power to walk the plank will significantly degrade so much so that he may indeed obey the compulsion of the imagination and actually fall.

Believe in Yourself

Bottom line: It is evident that in training for piano performance one must at the same time cultivate confidence in one's own powers. Without self-confidence, very little can be accomplished in any sphere of endeavor. You can do anything within reason. For instance: Your music memory is much better than you think. Neurologists know that there is no practical limit to the powers of human memory in general and musical memory in particular. Many of our great pianists have a repertoire of two or three hundred pieces, included among which are four or five concertos, say, a dozen sonatas, several works of the dimensions of Schumann's *Faschingsschwank aus Wien*, two or three of Liszt's *Hungarian Rhapsodies*, and perhaps 60 or 70 compositions, each of which takes eight or ten minutes to perform. These humans acquire this enormous repertory without any particular strain, and though, of course, some of them are specially gifted. There is no reason why the average musician who takes his work seriously should not at least memorize 50 works.

Long ago I set out to memorize poems. One a week or one every two weeks was my goal. Each night I spent 30 minutes going over the poem of the week. Now I can recite verbatim over 50 poems. Don't get me started. It sounds almost impossible, but after awhile committing to memory became second nature. The more you memorize, the easier it will become to memorize. Have faith in your own ability. Rewards will follow. Success is a great reward and rewards feed success. Try to prove that I lie.

American Memory Competitions

In the memory competitions held in New York City (March 2008), contestants memorized 99 faces and the associated names in 15 minutes. They memorized 30 25-digit numbers in 15 minutes and the order of a pack of 52 cards in just five minutes. These people are not freaks, geeks, or geniuses. They have, however, devoted attention to training their brains, their memories, and their attention spans, and so should you.

Walter Hilse, that conductor friend of mine, has pretty much memorized multiple operas and symphonies. He has the score before him, that's true, but it is there chiefly to give confidence rather than reference. Walter occasionally eyes the score, not so much to read it as to assure himself that his memory is not about to betray him. Only those of you who have examined a full orchestral score can form an adequate notion of the high degree of mental training required to memorize it and 50 more like it.

The Gift of Memory Is Nothing Special

This gift of memorizing music—especially when it is as highly developed as it is in our great conductors, pianists, singers, and memory athletes may seem a rare and special thing. Rest assured: It is not! Memory is one of the lowest functions of the human brain. Even idiots have it.

Even earthworms have it! Your cat and your dog have it. House flies have it. Our ancient ancestors needed it to find the berries and to recall where the hunting grounds were. Without memory and its continued improvement, our species would not have survived and you would not be here.

Basically, humans can have two types of memory: natural and artificial. The natural memory occurs automatically without much effort by just being alive and alert. Artificial memory uses tricks, peg lists, mnemonics, narration,—all sorts of tools to expand memory function and make us look like memory geniuses.

Let's Get Some Advice from an Expert—Ferruccio Busoni:

Although few are capable of analyzing artistic experience, one of the greatest has done so. "I have become convinced," writes Busoni, "as an old hand at this kind of thing, that playing from memory gives an incomparably greater freedom of expression. The player who is dependent on his notes finds this not only limiting but actually an interference. In any case, one must know the piece by heart if one is to give it the right shape in performance."

But if the printed music is actually an interference, why should so many, including experienced artists, be afraid of appearing on the platform without it? If the player, to interpret a work to the best of his ability, must possess the music, in the sense of knowing it thoroughly, why should he dread memory failure? Let Busoni answer: "Stage fright affects the reliability of memory. When it comes, your head gets confused, and your memory insecure."

Busoni speaks from experience, and he speaks truly: fear of forgetting is part of the problem of forgetting and that problem is due to nervousness, and the reason nervousness induces forgetting was explained. Do you recall why nervousness hurts memory?

Answer: nervousness creates a different brain state. And it was explained how to overcome break-down, nervousness, and forgetting. Stop now and review in your mind what you know and check your knowledge by rereading the appropriate sections.

If you don't believe brain state is important, try this experiment. Memorize a piece until you are sure you can play it effectively. Then imagine you are now at your teacher's home or studio and try to play the piece. See what I mean? Just imagining a different situation will often throw off your memory.

What Does Busoni Say About the Score Preventing Nervousness?

But here the issue is: Does the presence of the score necessarily prevent nervousness, does the score prevent disaster? According to Busoni "No." Even with the score up there with them, people break down and having the score is often no help because they have lost their place in the music. I have lost my place many times during a lesson and Ying had to tell me where I was. Has any real music student not had that experience?

Also, Busoni is of the opinion that the printed notes might prevent an obvious break-down, but they will not prevent the worst fault of all: Unmusical Playing!

But, You May Say, What if I Really Do Have a Poor Memory?

If you have trouble memorizing a Chopin waltz, don't assume you have a poor memory. An untrained memory—yes! But your ability to memorize is not likely to be below that of the average, and the capacity of the average memory is astonishingly high. But, alas, real achievement in music memory depends on training, training that can be hard work. Yes, work is involved, but not that much considering the results. The basic trick that memory experts use is to have an organized and associating framework on which to peg the information to be memorized.

Even the best memory expert and most expert musician cannot memorize a page of random notes. No sir! They, like you, need an organizing framework, a logical development of faculties, and the right appreciation of memory techniques, including pattern recognition, associations, narrative clues—all of which will quickly bring about astonishing results as you will soon see as you work through this project. Memorizing easy pieces will get easier and memorizing hard pieces will get easier. Don't believe me? Read on.

INTRODUCTION TO THE SCIENCE OF LEARNING

◆ ◆ ◆

Long ago, in Paris during the spring of a year that I am too lazy to look up, a young German (or was he Austrian?)—no matter—was standing at one of those book stalls by the Seine, the river that runs through that fair city. There and then, he picked up a book, the name of which is not recorded in his autobiography, and he read something. What he read is also lost to history. But at that moment, that man had a sudden flash of inspiration—an idea which changed the course of human history, an insight which has significantly changed my life for the better and which I hope will soon change your life for the better.

A Brief History of the Dawn of the Scientific Study of Human Memory

The idea was to study human memory scientifically. And to a scientist of that era (especially a German or Austrian scientist), the word "scientifically" meant quantitatively. By quantitatively, that man meant reducing memory to numbers by essentially measuring what was memorized and measuring what was forgotten and (more importantly) measuring when, why, and how it was forgotten.

Ebbinghaus, the Father of Modern Scientific Memory Research

The man was Hermann Ebbinghaus (1850-1909), a doctor of Philosophy and a genius. Hermann promptly returned home from Paris, kissed his wife, and then locked himself in his upstairs study to work on the complexities of human memory.

Hermann Ebbinghaus, 1850-1909, the first psychologist to study memory experimentally. He invented nonsense syllables, which he regarded as 'uniformly unassociated'.

Hermann Ebbinghaus (1850-1909), the first psychologist to study memory experimentally. He invented nonsense syllables, which he regarded as uniformly unassociated. Most textbooks will tell you that he got his idea of studying memory quantitatively from reading Gustav Fechner's book *Elements of Psychophysics* in London. But if that were true, why did Hermann not mention that in his autobiography?

HERMANN EBBINGHAUS' EXPERIMENTS

Using himself as the sole subject for his experiments, Hermann Ebbinghaus devised 2,300 three-letter nonsense syllables to measure memory. In a typical experiment, he would pick the nonsense syllables at random from a hat, review a list of 16 of these until he could recall them perfectly in two faultless executions aloud, and then retest himself at various time intervals, recording the results. All in all, he had 420 lists, and each took about 45 minutes to memorize. He estimated he did at least 14,000 repetitions. While the time spent memorizing the lists and the number of repetitions were closely correlated, Hermann found that the number of repetitions done was more important than the time spent. There are important physiological reasons why this is true, reasons we now know to be true, reasons that do not concern us here. In fact, the Nobel Prize in Medicine was awarded for the discovery of the brain mechanisms that underlie repetition as the major mechanism of learning. Just remember this: Neurons that fire together, wire together. And then, it follows as the night the day, neurons that are wired together will fire together. Key ideas like these are often more easily memorized as verse:

Neurons that fire together
Wire together
Neurons that wire together
Fire together

The lesson is clear: repetition counts. Repetition is an important part of learning and memory. Without repetition, very little learning takes place. Without repetition, very little learning can take place. Repeat this fact to yourself out loud so you are sure it is part of your understanding of the physiology of memory mechanisms in humans.

We repeat: repetition is important. Repetition causes neuronal networks to fire together and wire together, and once they do, they tend to be more easily fired together, the very process that underlies human memory. Therefore, develop a healthy and accepting attitude toward repetition. Repetition is good for you, and you should learn to enjoy it and not look down on it as a tedious, unrewarding activity. Attitude! "Right attitude," said the Buddha, "is good." And he was right.

OK, Hermann Locked Himself in His Room and Repeated Nonsense Words—So What?

So what? No way so what. You should be thinking: Wow! Think about it! Locking yourself in your study for three periods each day—10-11 AM, 11-12 AM, and 6-8 PM—for over four years and memorizing masses of meaningless lists. That's dedication, dedication to science. And mind you, all this must have been tedious and boring.

Must have been boring?

Yeeeahhh! What are we talking about? It was boring. Hermann says so in his famous book published at Leipzig in 1885, *Über das Gedächtnis*

(*Memory, A Contribution to Experimental Psychology*). Hermann, in confidential moments, admits that his brain loses its "freshness" after 20 minutes and becomes bored. When each test required longer periods of concentration, say—3/4 of an hour, he admits, "and toward the end of this time exhaustion, headache, and other symptoms were often felt which have complicated the conditions of the test."

One wonders how many headaches were generated to learn that lesson.

What Lesson?

Lesson: the human brain fatigues quickly. The human brain quickly loses its focus, becomes bored, and begins to shut down.

At-TEN-shun!

Failing to focus is one of the biggest things that interfere with memory and performance. You can't remember something that you didn't pay attention to in the first place. Think about this. It could be the reason you are not doing so well in piano lessons and in science class and in everything else that you are not doing well.

First, you have to get it; otherwise, you'll forget it. The best bet is to avoid boredom: Do a small amount of mental work at a time, take frequent breaks, and vary the subject matter—about those techniques, more later. Meanwhile, let's talk about what Hermann accomplished despite the boredom and despite the headaches.

Despite the headaches, the dull, dreary, mind-numbing humdrum, Hermann persisted. After he got an individual list memorized (as was mentioned), he retested himself at timed intervals and recorded what he recalled and what he did not recall. Along the way, he proved that human memory performance is a complex process that is time, modality, emotion, brain state, and brain lesion dependent. Some, not much, of the complexity will be covered later in this book. Despite the complexity, our man Hermann proved that memory can be measured exactly. His most important discovery, and the one for which he is very well known in psychological circles, was the "forgetting curve" that relates the amount of forgetting to the passage of time. That forgetting curve remains one of the eternal verities about human memory performance. There are other eternal verities about human memory, which we will cover, but that one—the forgetting curve—is among the most important. Never

ever forget the forgetting curve. Please always remember the forgetting curve.

Incidentally, there is also a learning curve. It is exponential, just like the forgetting curve, with the sharpest increase in learning on the first day. After that, the learning curve levels out much like the forgetting curve.

Time-Dependent Processes in Human Memory and Performance

There are two important time-dependent phenomena in human memory:

1. Forgetting and
2. Encoding.

Let's look at these items one at a time. Forgetting first.

Forgetting is the Default Mode of Human Memory

In a certain sense, the news about the forgetting curve ain't good: the default mode in human memory is to forget, and to forget quickly.

In the list of 16 nonsense words (like WUX, CAZ, ZOL, BAZ, etc.), for instance, which Hermann had memorized perfectly, only eight could be correctly recalled one hour later, and only five could be recalled after two days. Thus, overly learned material that had been recalled perfectly twice had slipped out of the memory at the rate of about one per cent per minute for the first hour. After two days, the rate of loss tends to settle down until a relatively constant level of retained information is reached two weeks later. Hence, if you can recall only a fraction of what you have read in the introduction to this book or a fraction of what happened to you two hours ago, don't fret or worry; your memory performance is quite normal. If you have played a piece perfectly twice, don't be surprised if you forgot half of it the next day. And don't be hard on yourself if, without review, two weeks later, you forgot 70% of it. That's the norm: 30% correct recall after two weeks and 70% forgotten under circumstances where memory tricks and associations have not been used. Yes, forgetting is the default mode of human memory.

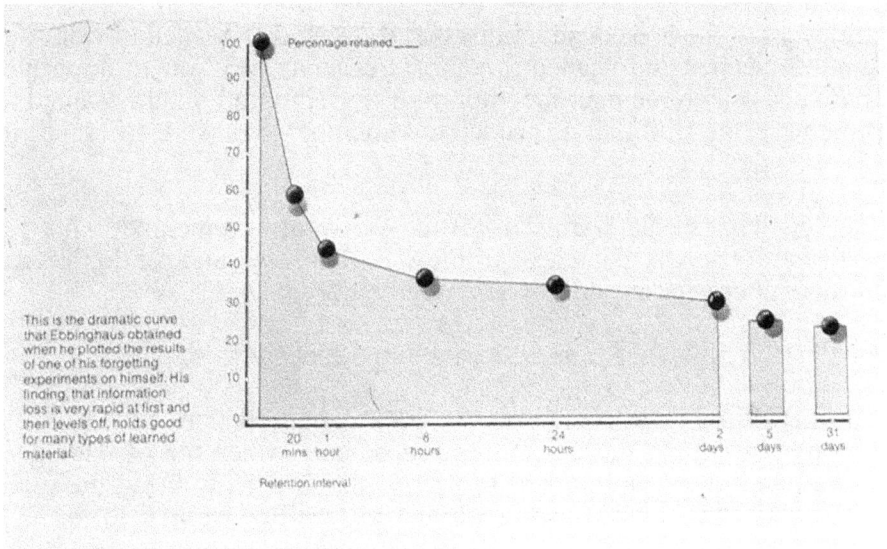

This is the dramatic curve that Ebbinghaus obtained when he plotted the results of one of his forgetting experiments on himself. His finding, that information loss is very rapid at first and then levels off, holds good for many types of learned material.

The forgetting curve for unassociated perfectly learned three letter items. Note the dramatic drop in retained material after just one hour. Within 24 hours over 60% is lost forever.

But What's the Deal? How Come We Forget So Easily? How Come We Have to Work to Remember?

Here's the answer: We need to forget almost everything. There are important reasons that our brains are biased to forget: most of the stuff we come into contact with in our everyday lives just isn't that useful, important, or memorable. Just think of what a nightmare life would be if you remembered every little detail of every little thing that happened every little moment.

"To remember everything is a form of madness."
– Irish proverb

A Russian psychologist, A.R. Luria, discussed (in an interesting book entitled *The Mind of a Mnemonist—A Little Book About a Vast Memory*) the case of S., who had the problem of not being able to forget. S. has a real name that is very long, very Russian, and almost unpronounceable, so S. is usually known to the psychological literature simply as S.

Yes, S. couldn't forget. He suffered the disadvantage of having a mind perpetually bombarded by past memories, most of which were irrelevant to the present situations that S. wanted or needed to work on. What S. needed and wanted in a most desperate way was to forget the trivia and only remember the important stuff, the stuff that he wanted to remember, the stuff that he needed to remember to make a difference in his everyday life.

We, too. That's what we need. Right? We want to remember what we want to remember, like a Mozart piece or *Fur Elise*, and we don't want to remember what we don't want to remember.

Goal #1: Forget trivia; remember the important stuff.

You bet. It's nice to remember the important stuff like your spouse's birthday, when the mortgage needs to be paid, when the garbage gets picked up, where you parked the car at the airport, to bring the math homework that you did to school, and to feed the cat, and so forth. A good memory can come in handy in many ways.

The trick is to remember the things that are important and forget what is not important. The techniques that are discussed in the pages coming up will allow you to do both (remember and forget) and give you control over your memory that you (perhaps) never thought possible. What will not be discussed is the form of active forgetting that psychiatrists see in people suffering from neurosis. In that form of illness, unwanted material is actively and unconsciously suppressed from the consciousness because the material tends to cause an unpleasant mental state called anxiety. The official psychiatric term for this kind of active exclusion of memories from the consciousness is repression. Repression is an exaggerated form of the normal tendency—but not an invariable tendency—for human nature to forget what is painful. We do so for the sake of peace of mind. Instinctively, we struggle for happiness, and in that struggle, we dismiss from our minds much that is hurtful. Repressed memories do tend to surface in dreams, during psychotherapy, and under the influence of drugs, particularly alcohol. Repressed memories usually have no direct application to music or music memory and therefore do not enter further into the scope of this book.

"What's too painful to remember, we simply choose to forget," sings Barbara Streisand. And she's right.

Repression May Cause Loss of Music Memory

In the realm of music, failures of memory are due to the same causes as they are in the circumstances of everyday life. Most pianists, even those of little experience, know what it is to interpret and perform a piece of music with the score not before the eyes and break down time after time at precisely the same place. There are various reasons for this failure (which will be discussed), but one reason is not that the music has suddenly become more difficult, but because their memory in that particular passage has failed them due to active repression. In the mind of the player, this particular passage of music may have associations with something that has been repressed and forgotten. The pianist is unconscious of the associations; nevertheless, because they exist, the pianist is prone to repress the music around which these repressed associations cluster.

For me, I have great difficulty playing or memorizing even simple pieces composed by the Russian composer Dmitri Shostakovich. I believe this difficulty is due to the associations that come forth when I see his name or read his scores. These negative associations derive from the rather negative impressions I have of Shostakovich during the time that I took care of him as his physician. What's the solution? I guess several years of intensive (and expensive) psychotherapy might rid me of my repressions and enable me to play his pieces. Or, I might handle the problem by just playing the pieces of other composers, of which there are many. That last solution works for me, even though it prevents me from playing the amazing Waltz No. 2. How you solve situations like this is up to you. In general, if you have a conflict and it is bothering you, the best treatment is to resolve the conflict so that it doesn't bother you anymore.

Another Problem: Some Parts of a Piece May Distract Us

For some reason, known only to God, at a particular part of the E minor section of the *Minuet in G* from the Anna Magdalena Notebook, my mind thinks of Sarah Palin, the Republican candidate for vice president of the United States. Something about the notes in measure three brings forth the Palin idea and the feeling that she was poorly qualified to be President and that tends to make me lose focus and foul up at that point in the piece.

Actually, why those notes summon the idea of Palin is not a mystery. My wife interrupted my playing exactly at that note cluster to tell me about McCain's ill-advised choice of Palin as a running mate. So, we could make a case that there was a temporal association of Palin with the notes of that section and that the two items (Palin and the E minor part in question) once associated in the consciousness each then recall the other. The evidence that this analysis makes sense is the fact that if someone tells me about Palin, I immediately recall the E minor part of the piece. Later, I will not explain how I get around this difficulty because I don't know how. The association is so fixed, probably because of the emotions involved, I can't shake it or suppress it. The memory association and the emotional tone (Palin not qualified to be president) are too firmly established to be erased easily.

Encoding

Human memory encodes in time-dependent stages. Most neuroscientists talk about a working memory that lasts for one and one-half minutes. (Some music books mistakenly say that this stage of memory lasts only ten seconds. That is completely wrong!)

Next, there is a short-term memory that lasts about two hours, and after that, there is a long-term memory lasting probably forever. The physical basis for the working memory is electrical activity in the brain, probably close to the frontal lobes; the physical basis of short-term memory is probably chemical changes at synapses with increased release of transmitters that facilitate synaptic transmission and a decreased release of inhibitory transmitters, which also facilitates transmission at the synapse. Most of that activity occurs in low midline structures of the brain.

With long-term memory, the actual memory trace is delocalized and stored diffusely and is based on the actual structural alteration of the brain with the growth of new synapses, the growth of more connections between nerve cells, and the production of new nerve cells, as well as the folding of special unusual proteins.

A detailed knowledge of the agencies that control these (quite complicated) stages of memory encoding and the subsequent readout of the memories for performance is not needed for you to use the information constructively in performing music tasks any more than a detailed knowledge of the (quite complicated) workings of the internal combustion engine is needed for you to successfully drive a car. But, in the hope that a not-so-detailed general knowledge of some memory mechanisms might help you memorize better, faster, and easier, here are the basic ideas related to the time-dependent encoding of human memories. I am covering these things here because I couldn't find them mentioned in any scientific way in any of the books I read on human memory or music memory.

Receptor Stage

All sensory modalities (smell, taste, touch, sound, vision, muscle position) have receptors that convert energy in the environment into electrical impulses which are then sent to the brain for reorganization and interpretation. Take the visual modality, for instance: Light hits the chemical in the eye which changes configuration and excites a retinal receptor which starts a chain of electrical impulses that eventually arrive at the brain. The retinal receptor does not turn off immediately. It continues to discharge for a fraction of a second, depending on the intensity of light and the situation surrounding reception. Because of this continuation of discharge after the stimulus is gone, we are able to maintain continuity of vision even when we blink and we are able to see moving pictures as a single continuous image even though multiple frames of the image are being projected. Thus, there is a very primitive stage of human memory that is based on receptor function and based in receptors. You can recall that this stage exists by remembering what happens when you prick yourself with a pin: The pain continues after the pin is removed, and in fact, you can exactly locate the place where you were stuck even though the stimulus (the pin itself) is no longer in your skin. The pain receptors are still discharging and that is why you can exactly locate where you were stuck.

As for me, I call this stage of memory the receptor stage and abbreviate this stage as R, where R stands for receptor, any receptor.

Stage I Memory or the Working Memory

Once information passes into the brain from the receptors it is processed in the working memory. The working memory is what we use to think. All conversations take place in the working memory. All conscious thinking takes place in the working memory. In the verbal working memory, the normal human can hold only seven items forward and five backward. So, if someone asks you to repeat the number 474-7670, you should be able to do so, and in the process, you will be using your working memory. If someone asks you to repeat the number backward, if you are like most people, you will have trouble and will only be able to repeat five of the seven digits backward.

The usual telephone system is built on this fact of working memory and that is why currently we have telephone numbers of seven digits. For some reason, the seven digits are more easily recalled if they are grouped into a group of three and four digits. Unfortunately, the working memory has a short term of existing, usually a little longer than a minute. That is why when you look up a number in the telephone book and prepare to dial it, you will fail if:

1. The period between look-up and dial without mental review of the number is significantly over a minute, or

2. Your attention is, just for an instant, focused on something else.

You will not fail to dial correctly if you say out loud or otherwise consciously rehearse the number until the number is dialed.

Performance of Any Music Requires Working Memory, Also Known as Stage One

All playing of music uses the working memory to read notes and play them and to play the piece by reading out of other stages of memory into the working memory. Because the working memory is based on brain electrical activity, the stage will be interrupted by a convulsion or by electric shock. In patients with severe dementia, this stage of memory is often preserved so a patient may carry on a reasonably coherent and fairly intelligent conversation, and yet if distracted, the demented person will be unable to recall what they were talking about, who they were talking to, or even where they were talking.

Stage One Memory is Preserved at Cocktail Parties

This stage, stage one, of memory is also preserved at cocktail parties, but other stages may fail due to the adverse effect of alcohol. Hence, someone may appear quite intact on the basis of small talk and carry on a reasonably coherent and fairly intelligent conversation, and yet when they wake up the next day, they will not recall anything about the party, much less what was said. Because the working memory is really the first stage of human memory, we refer to it as stage one, but other people may call it the "working memory" or the "ultra short-term memory."

Attention! Stay awake! A key point is coming. Are you still with me?

Stage One Memory is the Beginning of All Memories

If you don't go through stage one, you don't get to stage two or three. Therefore, to remember anything long term, you must conform to the requirements imposed on you by the biological imperatives and physiological limitations attached to stage one:

A. The to-be-remembered item must be consciously thought about.

B. The short duration of stage one and its limited storage capacity means that it is unlikely that you will be able to put into long-term memory items larger than the storage capacity of stage one, which is, as you recall, about seven items. This means it is unlikely that you will be able to memorize any piece of music except in small chunks. Sometimes that small chunk will be one measure with its complex structure, sometimes that chunk will be a sequence chunked by a category clue such as scale structure or cadence, or a repetition or a recognized chord. The seven-item limit applies to fingering. It would be hard to memorize the fingering for more than seven notes at a time. So, in general, keep the fingering to seven notes or less at a time.

About category clues and chunking and how to use them, more later. Meanwhile, just keep in mind that to memorize anything you must at first effectively deal with stage one. To memorize anything, you must pay attention to that thing long enough for you to become consciously aware of the thing itself and the number of items that you are aware of. The number of items to be placed in long-term memory must be about seven, no more, otherwise the probability of success is small. Indeed, the secret of learning music by heart, in view of the severe limitations of stage one memory, is to concentrate attention on one (small bite-sized) thing at a time.

Students who try to learn a dozen things at a time, changing fingering, and phrasing from day to day, or even minute to minute, and so forth, will get utterly bewildered. Is it surprising that some people fail to remember anything that they practice even though they practice a lot? They most likely are trying to memorize too much at once, and because of the physiological limitations imposed on humans by our biology, they fail.

THE CAUSE OF MOST MEMORY FAILURES
◆ ◆ ◆

Most memory failures are either due to inattention or too many items in the stage one memory (stage one memory overload). Reread the last sentence three times to firmly fix it in your memory. If you know the causes of memory failure, you will have a head's up on avoiding them.

About Natural Attention

Natural attention is also known as spontaneous attention. Complete concentration is typified by a child when playing a game he loves; so absorbed is he that, for the time being, nothing else exists for him. That animals have natural attention we can guess merely by watching a sporting dog on the scent of a rabbit or a cat stalking prey. Natural attention arises when the object (or idea or whatnot) upon which the mind is centered is associated with interest and enjoyment.

Older people, like myself, concentrate naturally for periods of time varying with the attraction of the thing attended to. Not only the lover, but the artist, scientist, and businessman, may experience moments (sometimes years) when emotion so intensifies interest that a person, idea, or ambition may become an obsession, occupying the mental field exclusively.

To practice your music with this kind of natural attention may not prove possible. But with willed attention (that is forcing your attention) on to the music, you should be O.K. And music itself will help focus your attention because it has movement, interest, enjoyment, emotion, sometimes passion, and most important of all: it sounds good.

Stage Two Memory

The next stage after stage one is (you guessed it) stage two. Others call this stage of memory "short-term memory" because it is based on the neuronal mechanisms that underlie short-term potentiation. To avoid confusion let's stick with our name and our terms.

Stage two is mainly chemically based and is needed to get information into the long-term memory. Thus, all the time-dependent processes must work in sequence for you to encode music in the long-term storage. First R (the receptor stage), then stage one (the working memory of consciousness), then stage two (short-term memory), and then stage three (long-term memory).

Notice how easy it is to recall the stages of human memory because they are the same as the sequence of numbers we all have all over learned by heart: one, two, three. All you have to do to look smart is remember to put the R in front of the one, two, three and remember what that R stands for. R of course stands for—?. Ye gods, did you forget receptors? Stage two memory is impaired by alcohol and other drugs, sickness, fatigue, and lack of adequate sleep.

Stage Three or Long-Term Memory

Stage three is also known as the long-term memory because it lasts a long time. It is the stage in which we would like our music pieces to reside. Regardless of the different names, the experts agree that long-term memory is physically based on long-term potentiation which is based (at least in part) on unusually folded brain proteins and on actual structural changes in the brain. Long-term potentiation and short-term potentiation are brain mechanisms based on brain biology, the details of which, though well understood, need not bother us here. If you really want to know about them consult Eric Kandel's book *Neuroscience* cited in the bibliography at the end of this book.

Summary of Key Information So Far

Most, if not all, memory failures are stage one failures—that is failures to encode in the first place due to poor attention or stage one overload.

Readout failures of information correctly transferred from stage one to two and three are due to ineffectively transferring information back from stage three to stage two, then to stage one, the working memory.

Most readout failures are due to the brain being in a different chemical state from the state in which the original memory was encoded or the operation of normal forgetting or forgetting by design or repression.

Failure of Stage One to Stage Two

When you forget where you parked your car at the airport, it is because you didn't force the information into stage two. So next time, just sit there for a fraction of a minute and tell yourself that here is where you parked. Note the surrounding and prominent landmarks that will help clue the memory when you return. Once you make a mental note of where you parked, try to forget where you parked. You can't!

When you walk into a room and don't know why you are there, that also is a stage one to stage two transfer failure. Next time, deliberately tell yourself, "I am now going into the kitchen to get the scissors." If you did do that, that is, if you actually consciously told yourself why you were going into the kitchen, then you may then think of anything you wish. When you get to the next room and ask why you are there, you will know. Don't believe me? Try it!

Most memory failures start with a failure to pay attention in the first place. Thus, most memory failures are due to failure to pay sufficient attention in the first place. You would be surprised how much information that passes into the working memory goes immediately out the window. How many times have you seen a traffic light? Yet are you sure which light is on top? How about when the lights are displayed horizontally? Which light is on the extreme left, red or green? Which way does Washington face on the dollar bill? If you are like most people, you have seen his face of the dollar bill thousands of times. And yet, and yet, you might not be sure which way he is facing. How many letters are omitted from the dial of your portable phone? From a dial phone? From your home phone? Which numbers on the phone are associated with four letters and not three? On the modern quarter dollar what is the order of print size of the words "LIBERTY," "THE UNITED STATES OF AMERICA," and "IN GOD WE TRUST?"

These things are not important, and I am not trying to beat up on you. Most people have seen these things repeatedly and most people don't care about them.

Most people don't care about the print size on the quarter, nor should they except recently "Liberty" has been degraded to much smaller print than on previous U.S. coins. Now "The United States of America" has the biggest print. What this means, I'm not sure, but it doesn't seem good.

You See a Lot by Looking

Yogi Berra famously remarked you see a lot by looking. That's true.

Unless you make a conscious effort to study and observe the details of your current memory piece, you are doomed to failure. Unless you make a mental note of where you parked your car, you are probably doomed to not remember where it is. Unless you make a conscious mental note of where to start the Mozart piece at that high Bb, you might not know where to start.

The Right Start is Key

Remembering where your piece starts is key to continuing the piece. Pay special attention to the starting point, including what notes are involved and how your hands are positioned on the keyboard, what they look like, and so forth. This sounds trivial, but it isn't. I myself in the beginning of my recital career had the heart-wrenching experience of sitting at the keyboard and not knowing where or how to start my piece. Don't let that happen to you. Beginnings are very important. Give them the attention they are due.

Each piece should be looked at with great attention to all the details displayed. You should consciously tell yourself the name of the composer, the key, the tempo, the time signature and so forth. Yes, talk to yourself. The words spoken, the movements of jaw and facial muscles will form associations that will help recall.

Look over the piece and look for scales, chord I, chord IV, and chord V, the most important chords. Before I start to memorize I play all the chords in the key. That tells me what to expect and what not to expect—two items that may help memory and recall.

Study the organization of the piece. Note patterns and repetitions. Is there any special form? Rondo? ABA? And so forth. You get the idea. General Patton, one of the greatest American Generals, famously said: "Time spent in reconnaissance is never wasted." "Reconnaissance always pays off big." Taking ten minutes to actually consciously and intensely study the music sheet without playing a note is good for your memory. Telling yourself (preferably out loud) what you are seeing will always pay big dividends. Studying the music before playing it is your form of reconnaissance. Do it.

Failure of Stage Three to Stage One is a Common Cause of Breakdown

You have already been given multiple ideas on how to avoid the problem and how to facilitate accurate read out of a stored memory from long term into the consciousness and the working memory of stage one. At this point it is sufficient for you to know that once the memory is in the long-term storage space (which we are calling stage three) it must, to be used, be called out and into stage one which is (as you remember) the working memory and the modality of consciousness.

Modern Memory Studies and Research

Since Hermann's (HE) original studies, over 10,000 memory studies have been done and hundreds of books have been written on the subject of learning and memory. We will now cover each and every one of these in great detail:

Only kidding, of course.

Even pseudo-scholars like myself wouldn't do that. Besides I am trying to write an interesting helpful book, not bore you to death.

Summary of Memory Truths

So here is a summary of memory truths to help you understand your memory and help you use those memory skills for better performance. Pay attention to these principles. They will give you a head up (and a leg up) on performance of any task that requires mental and physical work. As you read them, actively image or imagine how you might apply them to your current musical task. Recall the brain works best when it is doing and thinking. Another hint: Reread each of the principles each night just before you hit the hay. Reread them until (you guessed it) you can recite them from memory. Learn them as well as you learned the cycle of fifths or the major scales or the 31 chords. Without this foundation to build upon, no satisfactory progress can be made with this, or any other rational system. Time spent in review and repetition is never wasted.

The Neuropsychological Principles of Learning—Summary of the Principles of the Psychology of Learning

Review time.

Item 1: Time spent in review is never wasted. Multiple studies show that the students who do best are, by and large, the students who study. (Did you have any doubt about that?) Furthermore, the more you study, the more you learn. You get what you pay for: Spend the time and you will get the results. But don't overdo it. You don't want to develop a reputation for being a hopeless harmless drudge.

Ignacy Paderewski (1860-1941) famously remarked that if he missed a day's practice he would notice the ill effect of that omission on his playing; if he missed two day's practice, his wife would notice something wrong; and if three days passed without his touching the piano, the public would notice it. Paderewski had more than the usual problems with technique as we all know. But what worked for him (daily practice) might work for you. He claimed that the reason that he lost ability by missing just one day of practice was that his fingers got stiff. They may have stiffened alright, but not that much. The brain is especially equipped to rid itself of material that is not renewed on a daily basis. So, the effect that Paderewski noticed was more likely due to a degradation of brain engrams (memory traces) which directed the motor control systems assigned to move the fingers. The degradation would slow fingers and make them appear stiff. The problem, dear Brutus, is not in the fingers, but in the brain and in the nature of the forgetting curve. As discussed, the default mode of the brain is to forget and in fact there are active brain processes (recently discovered) specifically designed to promote forgetting.

Practice What You Need to Practice

Item 2: Also, don't forget you have to study the right material. If the French test is going to be on Chapter seven and you study chapter eight, you might not do as well as you deserve. In fact, Professor Hermann discovered that maximum efficient learning occurs when review time equals the exposure time to the same material. So, in general, for a one-hour lecture that you attend, you should spend one hour in review of that lecture. For the ten minutes it took you to read the last few pages in this book so far, you should spend ten minutes reviewing what you read.

Maximal Efficiency for Time Invested Depends on Review Time

Item 3: Yes, maximum effective learning occurs when review time equals learning time. What does that mean? If you are interested in maximizing the efficiency of what you learn, that is, learn the most in the smallest amount of invested time, the best bet is to review the material for the same time as the initial exposure. In the mental gymnastics course at Rice University, we have one 90 minute lecture a week. As this is the case, students should, for maximum efficiency, spend 18 minutes each weekday reviewing what was said in class. Recall that 18 x 10 = 180 / 2 = 90, the reason that it is suggested that the student take 90 minutes of review.

Notice there is no study on the weekend. The weekend is a sacred time. I wouldn't study on the weekend, so why should you? Rice students don't study on the weekend, most of them anyway. All work and no play make Jack a dull boy—Jill too. But I do practice on the weekends and so should you. One hour a day at the piano while you are seriously thinking about what you are doing will pay gigantic dividends. Try to prove I am wrong. You can't.

Item 4: Practice at least one hour a day every day. Make daily practice a habit. If you miss a day of practice I want you to feel bad about the omission.

More Time Usually Means More Material Mastered

Item 5: Because maximum efficient learning occurs when study time equals exposure time,it does not mean that more time will not result in more learning. The exposure rule is concerned only with getting the biggest reward for the smallest amount of time invested. The exposure rule is about efficiency of learning. The exposure rule is not about maximal mastery of material or total learning. It is not about proficiency. Proficiency is a horse of a different color. Proficiency will take much more time and many, many repetitions and reviews. Hard work but interesting work and for me at least FUN. Hence, if you had a one-hour piano lesson a week, maximum efficient learning (the highest rate of reward for invested time) would occur at one hour of review and the best and most efficient way to review would be to space the reviews at 12 minutes a day Monday through Friday. But mastery of the material would take much more practice as every real music student and every real music teacher knows.

Sickness Slows Learning and Makes Memory Defective

Item 6: Sickness and fatigue interfere with memory and learning by making our brains less alert and less effective. The reason for this is that the encoded memory traces are stored in a particular brain part called the neuron. Neurons are cells and when they are sick and tired they just don't work right. Sometimes neurons will respond to a short nap or a cup of java, but if you are really sick, just forget any serious mental gymnastics, music memory, or other mental tasks and concentrate on getting better.

How Associations Facilitate Recall—A Review

Item 7: Recall of memories is facilitated by association. In fact, once two items are associated in the consciousness, each one tends to recall the other. This is the basic principle of all human memory, which, believe it or not was discovered long ago by our ancient ancestors. It is the major way that long term, previously encoded memories are brought to the consciousness. Let's listen to the master about this:

"Ideas developed simultaneously or in immediate succession in the same mind mutually reproduce each other, and do this with greater ease in the direction of the original succession and with a certainty proportional to the frequency with which they were together."

Aristotle (384-322 BC)

Wow! What the ancients did not know could fill volumes. But in this case, Aristotle gets it right. But Aristotle did not make that discovery. He just talks about it. The real discovery was made in prehistory, somewhere and somehow, in a time out of mind—in a time older than the time of chronometers, when an unknown human learned that making mental images and associations of items and places facilitates recall and that two items, once linked in the consciousness, forever tend to help each recall the other, especially if the items are originally encoded in a visual and vivid way. This, friends, is the basic human mental mechanism behind memory and is the "discovery" that is at the basis of ancient and modern memory arts. The discovery, we can speculate, facilitated finding the berry patch after a long absence or finding the hunting grounds. Or knowing the safe place to build the teepee. In my view, memory of where the food was located played a gigantic role in the survival of our species. All humans have to eat. If they don't eat, they die. Thus, survival of our species was very much dependent on memory skills.

Associations—The Good, The Bad, and The Ugly

Associations are necessary to memory. And more than one neurologist and psychologist has noted that the brain is a coincidence machine: The brain remembers items that are coincidental in the consciousness. Two items once associated in the consciousness forever tend to recall each other. But what associations work best?

Associations that Get Our Attention Best are Those that Work Best to Preserve Memory

Associations are best when they are vivid, visual, violent, emotionally related to us and in motion. And as Aristotle notes above the more frequent the associations are made the more certain will be recall of one idea by the other. Associations that are cued by narration are an excellent tool for facilitating recall. The king died and then the queen died. What did the queen die of? Answer: A broken heart. Narration with a plot, a reason for an association, works best. The trouble is that you have to yourself think of the narration and the associations. Associations work best when you yourself make them up. Associations do not work best when someone else makes them up.

Our ancient Greek and Roman ancestors used to memorize immense amounts of material such as the entire *Iliad* and the *Odyssey*, which many of them could recite verbatim. Not only that. Saint Augustine tells us of his friend Simplicius who could recite Virgil's *Aeneid* backward! Simplicius used the ancient art of memory and I have no doubt that he could do this trick. In fact, many teachers in the ancient world did not consider that a student knew anything well unless they could recite the material backward. Forward recitation was not convincing enough.

The ancient art of memory was also used by musicians from the 12th century to the 16th century to memorize music. In fact, the music was often modified to facilitate the direct application of memory arts to the piece, not vice versa.

Be reminded the forgetting curve applies to unassociated meaningless triplet letter combinations. With association the curve is quite different and spread out over a longer time. Furthermore, it has been repeatedly demonstrated that once you memorize a piece completely and put it aside even for two years, relearning the same piece will take far less time and effort and the piece, once relearned, will remain in the memory much longer.

Task Specifics

Item 8: Active engagement is better than passive. If you want to learn how to touch-type, for instance, you should not take a course in which you merely watch others type. That is unlikely to get you anywhere. Remember the human brain learns best when it is actively involved in doing something that it is thinking about. Doing and thinking together—that's the ticket. The magic is in the mix of those two things. If you want to learn how to type, you have to get in there and think about typing while you are actually physically typing. Your piano playing will not be significantly improved by fixing your bike tire. Your piano playing is much more likely to benefit from (you guessed it) playing the piano.

Imagined Practice is Effective

Item 9: While active playing of a real piano is the best way of encoding music memory and performance, multiple studies have also shown that mental review is almost as good. While waiting in line at the supermarket, you can with profit go over your piece in your mind. Mental review can be visual with mental construction of imaged notes or it can be auditory with humming or tapping or singing. Or it can be a recited narrative that you devised to help recall the piece you are working on. Or you can hum or sing the melody. Mental review can be both visual and auditory. Objective tests favor visual methods of recall as they are proven to be more effective for most people. Try to make associations that have some visual connection. Recall the forgetting curve and the importance of review just prior to playback. Thus, instead of sitting dumbly on the bench awaiting your turn to go into the performance examination, you might profit by going over your piece, particularly its most difficult parts, in your head.

The Brain Gets Bored Fast

Item 10: Variety is better than a single task. Our brains get tired and bored fast. They are specially constructed to pay attention to anything that is new and different. That is why you will do lots better by varying the task at hand than trying to do the same thing over and over. It is better to read a non-fiction book for 15 minutes and then switch to a novel for 15 minutes and then switch back to nonfiction, alternating back and forth as you go. Each time you switch, your mind will be eager to get back to the other book before the usual ennui sets in or you begin to nod off. The net result is that you can often read two books in the same time that it would have taken you to read either book alone. Try this: Study two music pieces in the same sitting. Review one for ten minutes and then switch to the other. Keep switching back and forth. You should find that you learn both pieces more efficiently. Notice we said switch at ten minutes. This seems to be an important point. Your brain tends to fatigue at 20 minutes so you are better off stopping the project while your brain is still fresh and interested in that piece. The brain will then be eager to return to the interrupted task.

Currently I am memorizing Chopin's *Valse op. 64, No. 2*. When I feel my attention slipping, I switch to a different section of the same piece and approach that section with renewed vigor until I get tired of it and then I go back to the section I was working on initially and I am usually surprised at how interested I am in it again.

The brain has a mind of its own but techniques can trick the brain into remembering more material faster. Reminder: Each person's brain is different so the above advice applies in general, but not in particular. Some brains get bored in far less time than the 20 minutes stated by our friend Hermann and other brains actually never get bored no matter how much time is passing. What's true for your brain?

Proactive and Retroactive Inhibition

Item 11: Another thing to keep in mind about the above advice is a memory phenomenon called proactive and retroactive inhibition. This applies when two similar lists are memorized one after the other. The first list will tend to interfere with the recall of the second list (proactive inhibition) and the second list will tend to interfere with the recall of the first (retroactive inhibition). This phenomenon is not present when the lists are encoded using associative techniques. It is doubtful that in the course of memorizing two pieces of music one after another and alternating the tasks, that either of these memory processes (proactive and retroactive inhibition) will operate. If they do, or seem to, then just concentrate on one piece at a time. While I am talking about lists, I will mention the serial position effect.

Serial Position Effects

Item 12: When a list is memorized or a memory task worked on, the beginning and the ends are remembered best. In a musical piece, this means the center part may need more attention and work than the beginning or ends.

The Distributive Rule: Don't Cram—A Review

Item 13: Distribution of effort over time is important. If you are trying to learn how to touch type or tap dance or learn a foreign language, you are much better off and will achieve better results working one hour a week for 40 weeks than, say, working eight hours a day for five days. The evidence for the benefits of distribution of tasks is overwhelming, but doesn't concern us here. It is simply true and will remain true on this planet for the next 4.5 billion years when our sun will become a super red giant and burn Earth to a crisp. Scientists hope, by the time that happens, humans will have emigrated to another solar system to pollute another planet.

Stop!

Think for a while and discover for yourself why and how you recognized the above repetition about humans leaving Earth. What was it about this repetition that got your attention and made you aware that you had encountered that idea before?

What's the lesson? Little bits over a long time are much better than a lot of material all at once. In other words: Don't cram!

With the distributive rule in mind, determine which approach is likely to result in the most music progress if you have two hours to devote to music and one hour to do housework:

Answer A: Do the two hours of music first, then do the hour of housework.
Answer B: Do the hour of housework, then do the two hours of music.
Answer C: Do one hour of music, then an hour of housework, then an hour of music.

Notice: Those morons who did not circle answer C or otherwise know C is the answer, must go directly to jail and not pass Go.

A recent proof of the distributive rule came from an experiment done by the British postal system. They switched over to postal zone codes that have letters and numbers and had to train their workers to touch type. Touch typing can be tested in a standard way as those of you who took typing in school know so well. The postal officials divided the employees into groups. One group worked one week for 40 hours and another group worked one hour a week for 40 weeks. The group that distributed the learning task, namely the one hour a week for 40 weeks group, was the overwhelming winner, proving it doesn't pay to cram.

What Does State Dependent Learning Mean in Relation to Music Memory and Performance?

Stop here and answer the question recalling as much as you can. Then read on and grade your answer. How many important points did you cover? Grade yourself. Most people will recall only three items and that gets a C+.

Item 14: State dependent learning means that for maximally effective recall the brain must be in the same physical state or a state that is similar or reasonably similar to the state it was in during the actual learning process. Otherwise, there may be problems. Also, it is a good idea to store your piece in both your conscious and subconscious mind. Traditionally, memorizing music is done by playing through a piece repeatedly until it becomes automatic. Musicians who practice this method rarely attempt to put the music also into their conscious mind or awake mind. This is what as known as rote memory. Thus, the music exists in the artistic and expressive part of the motor brain and is subconscious. During a performance, when the pressure on the musician is great, it might be difficult to stay subconscious, where the music was memorized. If the brain shifts to the other state—the conscious state—where the music is not located, the performer will think he/she has gone "blank." He/

she will think that they have gone blank because (what else?) they have gone blank.

State Dependent Learning is Real and Really Important

Most performances will benefit from simulated performance before a group to try to duplicate the setting of recital. Wearing the same clothes that you intend to wear for the recital and having the same chemical brain state would also help, as mentioned. For instance, if you learned your piece and practiced it most mornings at ten AM after you drank two cups of coffee at 8, then your best performance would be under the same exact conditions ten AM and two hours post two cups of coffee. If the recital will use a real piano, practice on a real piano and not on a keyboard, and so forth. Pay as much attention to your performance during rehearsal as you would during performance. At your rehearsal and at your performance no one should be listening more attentively to the music that you are playing than yourself. During rehearsal imagine yourself before a large audience. Picturing that scene in your mind's eye will go a long way in overcoming recital jitters.

Review Time:

Anxiety and stage fright alter brain chemistry and electrical activity of the brain, often placing the brain in a state that is different from the brain's state during practice. Thus, during anxiety, playback conditions differ from learning conditions. Consequently, there may be trouble.

Some of the recital difficulty stems from anxiety changing the brain's chemical state such that the brain's condition during performance no longer matches the brain's condition during learning. Hence, inexperienced pianists are often surprised that during recital they flub the piece they did so well so many times at home. The treatment for this is varied and has been covered.

How to Cope with Recital Fear

Experience helps calm recital fears. Good teachers do the same. Overlearning of the piece helps too. Learning the piece under multiple conditions of brain function will also help. Repeat the piece when tired, when wired from too much coffee, when unhappy, and when elated. Repeat the piece whenever you can before whatever audience you can drum up. Repeat the piece on different pianos and at different times of the day and night. It is also important to repeat the piece under conditions of interruption, because interruptions (usually a cell phone) may occur during recital and it is better to be prepared for such a contingency than not be prepared. The idea is to encode the musical information sequences at several levels of brain states and conditions.

Sometimes Even Experienced Performers Need Tricks

If tricks are needed, experienced performers will use them. In 1926, George and Ira Gershwin mounted a show called *Oh, Kay!*, with Kay played by a frail and not-altogether-confident Gertrude Lawrence. Although *Oh, Kay!* was fluff, it produced one of Gershwin's greatest songs, *Someone to Watch Over Me.* Lawrence was too nervous to effectively deliver *Someone to Watch Over Me* before the large audience. George Gershwin saved the song from being dropped from the show by instructing Lawrence to sing it to a sad-looking doll instead of to the audience. Forget the audience and sing to the doll. The original presentation of the song brought boos. The new presentation brought standing ovations. The trick was that by singing directly to the doll, Lawrence was able to screen out the audience and concentrate her full attention, heart and soul, on the performance. Use the same trick when you can: Concentrate your full attention, heart and soul, on the performance and screen out the audience as best you can.

What Happened to Gertrude Lawrence?

Friends, those of you who suffer stage fright, despair not. There's hope. Three decades later, Gertrude Lawrence played the female lead in Rogers and Hammerstein's *The King and I.*

I know pianists who handle the stage fright problem in the same way that Lawrence did. They concentrate completely on the piece and thereby mentally isolate themselves from everything else in this wide world including the audience. What works for them might work for you. My best performances have been when I was so totally involved with the music that I was almost unaware of the audience.

Other Tricks

The Norwegian composer, pianist, and conductor Edvard Grieg controlled his anxieties by carrying with him three mascots: a red troll, a pig with a four-leaf clover in its mouth, and Grieg's lucky frog. Grieg's favorite was the frog, which he carried in his coat pocket when he conducted or performed. Before stepping onto the stage, he would put his hand in his pocket and rub his lucky frog. And he always had the troll and the pig on his bedside table. According to Nina, his wife, he always said, "Good night" to them. This sort of thing works if you believe in it and won't work if you don't.

Pause for a Brief Sidebar About Lesson Jitters

Lesson jitters are similar to and different from stage jitters. How many times have you been able to play a piece straight through from memory at home and yet failed rather quickly during your lesson with the teacher? If that problem doesn't sound familiar to you, you haven't taken enough lessons or memorized enough pieces.

My explanation for this commonly experienced phenomena is threefold.

First, there might be the state dependent effect because, after all, practice alone and play before the teacher are two different things. And two different things will have two different brain states.

Second, perhaps, there is the element of fear and anxiety in the lesson situation. Certainly, fear and anxiety play a role early on, but as time goes by most students love their teacher and have little fear. With my first teacher, Miss Platz, I was too young and too stupid to be afraid. With Madge, I was afraid and often had a pain in my stomach because I knew within the first minute of my playing, Madge would shout "Stop!" and explain what I did wrong. Jimmy and Ying never ever caused lesson jitters.

Third, in this setting under the scrutiny of the teacher, there are interruptions of the motor sequence. The usual scenario is that the student starts to play and the teacher notices a wrong finger, a misplaced note, or wrong rhythm, or some mistake or the teacher tries to steady the rhythm by playing in a higher register or playing on another piano or the teacher starts to hum or vocalize to help steady the student's playing. In other words—the student is interrupted with the aim of improving the situation. But, of course, the motor sequence is broken in the process and the performance gets flummoxed.

The real damage is that the student has not been permitted the freedom to try to play through. The student has not been permitted even the semblance of a partial success. Failure to succeed is a serious problem and is often the root cause of future failures. In general, failure breeds failure and the reverse is also true: success breeds success.

Practice playing from memory should simulate playing from memory conditions in every way including NO INTERRUPTIONS. During the actual recital, the teacher wouldn't dare interrupt the performance. After the student has gotten through the piece, there will be plenty of time to correct faults.

Conclusion:

When the student is asked to play their piece in the studio, they should not be interrupted. They should play through as best they can. Then, and only then, should the teacher go over the mistakes one by one.

1. This policy will build confidence because the student will have proven to himself/herself that they can get through the piece because, after all, they did. They may not have been note perfect or rhythm perfect or fingering perfect or perfect in any way, but they did get through. Anyway, few human things are perfect. General George S. Patton said, "A good plan today is better than a perfect plan tomorrow." My view: A good performance today is better than a perfect performance at some future time.

2. This policy of letting the student play through will give the student excellent practice in how to cover mistakes and continue on. Covering mistakes can make a gigantic difference in how the audience perceives the performance.

True confession: As I have become an expert at covering mistakes (because I make lots of them), the application of coverage techniques will be handled in Part II. In general, it is much better to cover mistakes or disregard them, than to stop or shake your head "no," or to apologize for the errors. I repeat: NO excuses! NO apologies! NO stopping! Play on as if everything is OK, smile, shake your head "yes" and the audience will think that everything is OK.

General Rule: Do Not Start Again

Starting again is an admission of error and is sometimes interpreted by the audience as a discourtesy. It is often better to continue on than pause and start again.

Furthermore, starting again doesn't guarantee success and indeed starting again may result in the same failure at the same place, a blackout, which is usually due to too much reliance on kinesthetic memory (to be discussed later in detail).

Rather than start again, preplan a place ahead of the trouble spot so that you can jump over the trouble spot and land on the prefigured place of rescue.

As for me, I usually have multiple spots in the piece that I can skip ahead to. But don't tell your teacher I said you can skip ahead: Here now for the record (and only for the record) I advise that you really should not skip anything. But, you know, this is an imperfect world and desperate situations call for desperate measures. So, if you do blank out, skip ahead to the part you know, your lifesaver. These spots I call life savers, as their employ does seem to save the performance from looking bad. Was it not Liszt who said, "Never mind the wrong notes—Play!"

Memory is Modality and Task Specific

Item 15: Memory and learning are task specific. Old Chinese motto: Want bean? Plant bean. Want corn? Plant corn.

Focus your attention on the things that will count and focus your attention away from the things that won't count that much.

Question: With the task specific memory principle in mind, what task should you concentrate on if you wish to become a pianist?

Answer: Playing the piano.

The Brain Sorts Items on the Basis of Similarities and Differences and Amount

Item 16: Analysis of similarities and differences enables you to make the associations that facilitate recall. Aristotle pointed out that the best way to compare things is by analysis of the similarities and differences. This is the basis of the high school English essay "compare and contrast." It is also the basis of our present scientific classification of plants and animals. The similarities are represented in the genus and the differences are in the species. But what happens if things are exactly the same? How do we compare then?

Again, our friend Aristotle has the answer: We compare things that are the same by measuring amount. For instance, Aristotle tells us that one talent (an ancient unit of money weighing about 50 pounds) is the same as another. That makes sense because we know one dollar is the same as another. So, to compare one pile of money with another, we count. By the way, Aristotle, master of those who know, gives it for his opinion that it is better to have more money than less. Most people would agree. But talking about money reminds one about spending. (Notice how the brain associates money with spending.) The idea of spending reminds us that we are spending time on similarities and differences and amounts because those are the analytic tools that give us a handle on the associations that will facilitate specific recall of memorized passages in memorized pieces of music. When you get a repetition, repeat it. When the repetition is different, note the differences and remember them.

Make Associations that Facilitate Recall

Remember that our Doctor Ebbinghaus noted early on in his studies that association facilitates recall. The reason for this is that once two items are associated in the human consciousness each tends to recall the other. His idea is of great importance for those of us who want to memorize something as abstract as music, for music exists in the ether. Music is not solid like a stone or a piece of wood. It is an abstract art form, probably the most abstract art form on this planet. For our minds to get a hold of it, we need to have some concrete hooks. Associations can provide such hooks, as the next volume of this project will show with the direct application of association techniques to memorizing some music.

How the Brain Does its Work and How to Make it Work Better

Essentially the human brain is a coincidence machine: When two items are viewed closely together in the consciousness, they recall each other and they usually do so in the ordered sequence in which they were first associated. If you think this is not true, try reciting the alphabet backward. You will find it is harder, much harder, to recite the alphabet backward, than to recite it forward. It also follows that if you can recite the alphabet backward, you will be able to recite it forward for, if the harder task is possible, the easier is also possible.

Your Memory is Much More Powerful Than You Think

Need another example of the power of these techniques? Scipio, the famous Roman General, knew by heart the three names (given name, family name, acquired name) of each of the 32,000 troops in his army. It's a good thing he did. Because the effectiveness of his personally knowing his troops led them to defeat Carthage in the battle of Zama in 202 BC, ending the second Punic War. If Rome had not defeated Carthage, this book would have been written in Punic and not in a language based on Latin.

The point: If our ancient ancestors could perform such gigantic memory feats with memory training, it shouldn't be difficult for you to memorize a little piece by Mozart or Beethoven.

The Human Brain is a Powerful Thinking Machine

Most neurologists agree there are no physical limits to the amount of material that the human brain can remember. There are excellent structural reasons why this is so, but detailed discussions of anatomy and physiology and brain organization are beyond the scope of this book. It is enough for you to believe that your brain is the most powerful thinking and memory machine on this planet, because it is. Amazing, right! And even more amazing is the fact that over 90% of the human brain is made of water. It's hard to imagine serious thinking and effective memory coming from something made mainly of water.

Make Your Own Personal Associations

Our ancient ancestors and the masters of the modern schools of memory like Harry Lorayne teach us that most associations work best when you yourself make the associations. The associations do not work as well when you are using someone else's association. Also it pays to build the new material, which you don't know and are trying to learn, on old material that you do know and know well. In fact, the more you know, the more you can know by building new associations on what is already solidly in your mind. In memorizing music, there will be as many associations and methods of association as there are individuals. There is no single way to approach a music task and the one we choose may not be the only or even the best strategy despite our attempts to get the facts and completely encompass the data. But in general the associations that will work best are those that are firmly based on what you know recognizing similarities and differences between what you know already and what you are trying to learn. Thus, if you know your scales, chords, cadences, and rhythms, you will do better than if you didn't know them because your associations will be richer and more numerous. How much easier is it to remember to play a C triad chord sequence than to try to remember to play C-E-G as individual notes in that order?

Names and Labels, No Matter How Strange or Ridiculous, Help Encode Memory

There was a certain part of a Mozart piece that I had difficulty getting into my memory. When my teacher Madge called this the unusual chord, bingo! I now had a label and an association by which to recall this chord. In fact, the unusual chord now stands out in my memory as the landmark in the piece. Madge pointed out the relation of this unusual chord to what was happening in my other hand and the fact that the chord appears nowhere else in the piece. The part of this music that used to give my memory trouble now had a local habitation, a name (the unusual chord), and a unique existence—plenty of reasons for me to remember it by multiple associations. Notice the brain does not suffer from multiple associations. On the contrary, multiple associations facilitate encoding and will subsequently facilitate recall.

Narrative, narrative, narrative—tell yourself a story to help yourself remember. Do it in your own words in your own way. If need be, make up your own words to go with a wordless piece that you are playing.

Sometimes Illogical and Imaginative Stories Can Easily Jog Our Memories

How this happens is that the items in the story are easier to recall than the items to be recalled and it is the link in the story of the easy item with the hard item that facilitates the memory. Experts in education find that a powerful way to learn is from stories. We seem, as human beings, to respond profoundly to narratives, and to extract from certain tales key items that are useful.

For example, memorize this number: 738613572722. Not easy, right?

Now memorize this story with a map of Manhattan in mind:

73 Trombones led the big parade across 86th street. When they reached 13th Avenue they turned left and they met 57 clowns who were distributing 27 ice cream cones to 22 Dallas Cowboy Cheerleaders.

Memorize the story and then turn aside and write the number by telling yourself the narration of the events in time.

Chances are that I can do this easier than you can because I lived in Manhattan until I was 30—until I was drafted into the Vietnam War. Thus, I am a native there and to the manner born. I have a map of Manhattan in my head, the way some musicians have a picture of the *Moonlight Sonata*. I can make pictures in my head of 86th street and 13th Avenue. And I have no trouble seeing clowns and those luscious Dallas Cowboy Cheerleaders. The associations are not logical but they are my own and thus I will have a further advantage. If you made up your own narration starting with the number 73, your narration would work better for you than your narration would work for me. But chances are you didn't even bother to make up a story. You were too eager to push ahead into something that was less work and easier. Too bad! If you didn't do the story, you missed out on actually proving to yourself that a narrative technique helps recall of specific information.

Narrative Notes

Here's how I kept oriented when I played *Blues in the Night* at Ying's recent studio recital: I studied the music. I broke it down into separate parts. I named each part and I sang the whole song several times. Thus, I have firmly associated the words of the song with my performance on the piano to good effect. I am using the melody of the song and the words as pegs on which to hang the memories needed for effective performance.

True confession: During the recital, I was actually singing the song under my breath. The point I am making here is that it is possible to memorize a piece by making associations and using the associations as peg items onto which the memory is hung.

How Does the Place System Work?

In the Greek and Roman versions, there are two sets of images. First, one memorizes in advance a set of images. This is the laborious part of the method and the reason that I (Dr. Patten) prefer peg systems based on familiar numbers or letters of the alphabet. Cicero used the pictures in his home and in his imagination walked through his house to view the images each in turn. He did this over and over again and checked the results with an actual walk until he could picture all the images in his mind in the correct sequence.

Next comes the second stage of the procedure. Supposing Cicero wanted to memorize the main points of a speech, he would form a second set of images symbolizing these points. The image symbolizing the first point would then be superimposed on the image of the first place, and so on. When Cicero wants to recall what's next, or even what he was talking about at the moment, he will run through the set of places in his mind and find the superimposed images. He might even say as he is recalling the images, "in the first place." And then when he wished to recall the item or idea that was next, he would think, "in the second place" and so forth.

Cicero will not and cannot look at the whole panorama of images all at once, but will review each in turn as if he were walking through his house. Suddenly, says Cicero, the item to be recalled will be "donated" to him by the primary image to which the to-be-remembered item was attached. Students should not be surprised by the effectiveness of the system when they realize how vividly the images are encoded with each other. The basic principle of human memory being that once two items are connected with one another in the consciousness, each tends to recall the other and in that order. The more vivid, the more interesting, the more colorful, the more unusual, the more violent, the more tightly the items will be associated with each other in the mind and the more likely that each will recall the other.

The same set of images can be used to memorize a different speech or a poem, or a set of the 50 names of the men in your army or all the different sections of the *First Viennese Sonatina* by Mozart in the exact sequence of the sections as they occur.

Cicero considered the initial set of images a kind of wax tablet which can be reused by merely blotting out the previous things written on the tablet and writing something new over it. Once one has made the effort to fix the initial set of images in the mind, one can use the same set of images any number of times.

If all this seems vague and useless, think again. Use parts of your home to memorize any sequence you wish. Prove to yourself that the system Cicero recommended does actually work. I know most of you out there in reader land won't bother to test the system for yourself. That is your loss.

What is the Point of Having Two Sets of Images? Why Not One?

Two sets have a number of advantages, including the ability to recall items in order or in reverse order or in any order whatsoever. This is why Seneca was able to recite the verses in reverse order: He just ran through his house backward. This is the reason Saint Augustine's friend, Simplicius, could recite Virgil's *Aeneid* backward. He just worked backward through the enormous imaginary buildings and rooms he used to memorize the poem forward.

Using the place system, Cicero can not only recall the points in his speech but also the order he wanted them presented. He can also select an item and look to either side to see the point before that item and the point after. The background images also can supply a connection and association that might otherwise be difficult to recall.

It is easy to see how the place system could be used to remember a dozen items or 20 names. But how could it be used to remember 2,000? Answer: Some of the ancients had over 100,000 places to store items. Whatever we may think of this figure, Harry Lorayne had that many places and more to store the entire Manhattan telephone book. Quintilian mentions that Metrodorus had a set of 360 places probably for eristic arguments and could hang several items onto each place. *Rhetorica ad Herennium* tells us flatly that, if we want to remember many things, we shall have to prepare many places.

At this point, you might think about the place method and consider how you might apply this powerful technique to help you organize your performance of a long and difficult musical composition. The next volume will illustrate the practical applications of this kind of visual associations.

Meanwhile, consider this question: How are the stations of the cross displayed in Catholic Churches used as memory tools? Why does this work? What is accomplished?

Narrative Sequence Can be Illogical

Recall that Harry Loraine got from the number 13 to the image of riding up to the gas station by a sequence of imaginative but illogical steps: 13 → tm → tomb → driving a tomb to fill up more → Fillmore. That is how I do it. Others use abecedarian lists—lists that follow the order of letters in the alphabet. That's OK too. These people tell themselves this is part A of the piece, this is part B, now I am back on part A again with the variation that ends the piece, and so forth.

Example: Eric Satie's *First Gymnopédie* (in D major and Dorian Mode although the key signature is C) begins after a four-measure intro with an eight-measure melody (A), which is repeated with a modification and extension of one measure (A'). B and C follow as two five-measure phrases and then eight measure D moves to cadences at measures 38 and 39. Thence follows A, A', B, C, again (thank God for exact repeats—listeners love them and so do we performers). F in measure 72 introduces another small change, etc. along to D' which concludes with a cadence identical with 38 & 39. Thus the form is A, A', B, C, D, A, A', B, C, D'. Cool, right? And not hard to recall as ABCD is a sequence we all are well familiar with and will not forget. Also notice how the larger pattern is even easier to recall: It's double A's BCD times two with the last D a little different.

Other people will use numbers and letters: This is part I of the two parts of A of the minuet, and so forth. As for me, I use everything I can think of or imagine—numbers, letters, stories, whatever. I need all the help I can get.

Your mind is a channel for reaching worlds beyond the material objects of everyday life, through imagination. The mind offers us a means of bringing an abstract world such as the abstract world of music into Technicolor reality.

Example: In performing *Blues in the Night* (Words by Johnny Mercer, Music by Harold Arden) I have a map of each section in my head with a name for the major parts. The first part is "My Mama done tol' me" as the music seems to duplicate the song words. The first riff sounds like train whistles so I call it the train section. The second riff is nightingale as that is how Julie London sings it. After nightingale, the cadence section reminds me to go back to "My mama" and that leads directly into the coda which Arden has labeled as such. Having these labels available for the mind, just as Cicero had places in his home available for his mind, makes it hard to get lost in the piece and even harder to play train before nightingale and coda before them both.

Face it, sequences are a part of our everyday life. Breakfast first, then lunch, then dinner, then dessert. Monday, then Tuesday, and so forth. Orgasm, but foreplay first.

The naming of musical sections and the naming of the sequences gives a degree of conscious control of the material and is part of the technical repertoire employed to activate explicit memory and provide the correct chords, notes, and sequence. One of the major scientific discoveries of the last century was the properties of explicit memory versus the properties of implicit memory. The exploitation of these properties is to use them both in your performance. But what are explicit memory and implicit memory? How do they differ?

EXPLICIT MEMORY AND IMPLICIT MEMORY

Explicit memory is under conscious control, while implicit memory is not. Explicit memory is very dependent on language, and implicit memory is not. This dependence is not a coincidence, as language and conscious awareness are closely linked phenomena. We use explicit memory when we explain how to play a C triad and implicit memory when we play that chord without consciously thinking about it. Implicit memory is also used when we ride a bike or do anything automatically, like tying shoelaces.

Most human cognitive processes use implicit memory to function without language or even consciousness. Any physical activity, such as playing tennis, walking, running, eating, and drinking, largely occurs automatically—without a verbal running commentary on what to do next. Have you ever had a solution to a problem pop into your head? That's a clear example of thinking about that problem taking place at a level other than self-aware consciousness. Indeed, most neuroscientists believe spoken language is merely an afterthought of more fundamental, preconscious cognition. Watch yourself next time you buy an ice cream cone. You will know what flavor you want before the word for that flavor appears in your mind.

Explicit Memory and Implicit Memory—Use Them Both

The key task in music memory and performance is to get the piece into implicit memory while using explicit memory to stay on track, recover from implicit memory failure, and give overall shape to the performance. Yes, this is the key task of music memory, but remember the key task of performance is to maintain a sense of musicality, without which none of the masterpieces can be played well.

Use language to shape elements of thought and performance in a way that the mute mind cannot. Use both explicit and implicit memory in performance and in trying to memorize a piece. But never forget your first duty is to be musical. Do not remove the muse from your music.

What Methods and Techniques Should You Use?

Use what works for you. Remember, one size doesn't fit all. Some students do better with visual mnemonics, others with sounds, and some by telling themselves ridiculous stories. Most students will find that some tasks are easier with one method and harder with another. Some pieces seem easier to memorize with one method or one set of associations than with another. Some pieces are easier to memorize just by memorizing the pattern sequence of notes and nothing else. For instance, in Debussy's *Le Petit Nègre Cake Walk*, the same pattern repeats, starting first on high E, then on C, and then on A. Once the sequence is learned, you can play it right by just recalling the A minor chord and working down. The same sequence repeats by starting in low E and working down A minor again.

There are many ways to skin a cat and many ways to memorize music. Remain open-minded, flexible, and practical. Experiment to find out what works for you and what doesn't. Then act accordingly.

Pattern Recognition

If possible, try to recognize a pattern and use it to get around the seven-item limitation of human memory. Consider the following letters. Try to memorize them. I think you will find this hard: LFAPOGAICIBF. Now memorize the same letters grouped into a meaningful pattern: FBI CIA GOP AFL.

Sequences and Repetitions Are the Similarities and Differences of Music

Recognition of sequences and repetitions provides major pattern associations that facilitate recall. In the case of a usual piece, I organize my memory items by numbers that relate to rhythmic groups. When I want to recall the rhythmic group, I first recall the number, which in turn helps recall the group. The message here is that the brain assimilates information that has been packaged into easily understandable patterns and groups. The brain likes easily digestible (small) pellets of information; it does not like chaotic gaseous clouds. Another mnemonic I use is to recognize the main melodic idea or ideas of the piece. These are usually stated in the first few measures and then repeated throughout the piece at different pitches and in modified form. Even when modified, they provide a musical landmark in the landscape of the piece. By recognizing where they are similar and different, I can make a mental map of the music. I am trying to convert the complex cloud of musical information into something patterned and compact enough for my brain to handle.

Example

Give yourself one minute to memorize this number: 17761812186119191941. Did you spend one minute looking at the number? Now turn away and write the number in the correct order. Hard, right?

Now try to memorize the number knowing that it is composed of the years that the United States was involved in major wars:

1776—Revolutionary War
1812—War of 1812
1861—Civil War

PIANO BY HEART

1919—World War I
1941—World War II

Now recall the number by recalling the wars, the order of the wars, and the years of the wars. Notice how easy things get when there is organization to the material that you wish to recall.

This phenomenon (remembering items by placing them in groups) is known to psychologists as chunking.

Here's another example of chunking: Take three minutes to memorize this list: Jail, Face of Evil, Delphinium, Beam of Light, Egg, Horse of Course, India, Candle, Apple, Grandchildren. Now get a piece of paper and write all the items you recall. Record the result. A normal person will get two correct. People reading this book are not normal, so we will expect a better result. If a large group of normal people are tested, the correct items will tend to be the first items in the list and the last items in the list. This phenomenon, in which we tend to recall the beginning and end and forget the middle, is called the serial position effect.

Musically, we must compensate for this serial position effect by giving special attention to the middle of our piece, as we will tend to better recall the end and the beginning of a piece than the middle. Usually, the beginning gets the most practice, so that usually beats the end. Therefore, the priorities in the usual piece would usually be to study the middle more than the end and the end more than the beginning. In fact, in informal discussion with some music teachers, I discovered that some of them recommend starting your memory task at the end and then doing the beginning and the middle. Experiment and see what works best for you.

Now memorize the same list for one minute by encoding the items according to the first letter of the item. There are ten items, and each starts with a letter A to J. Tell yourself, out loud, A is apple, B is beam of light, C is candle, etc. Don't worry about encoding, and don't make mental images, just say it. Go through the entire list. Remember you are trying to prove something to yourself.

A is apple
B is beam of light
C is candle
D is delphinium
E is egg
F is face of evil (it might help to visualize an evil face with this item)
G is grandchildren (see a grandchild in your mind's eye)

H is horse of course (note that the rhyme helps recall of the complete item)
I is India (OK—picture it)
J is jail (picture yourself in jail)

Now turn away again and write what you recall. Your score should improve because you are now attaching the new information (the items) to a systematic set of pegs that you already know (the letters A, B, C, etc.). If you have trouble doing this, remember to be systematic. The letters of the alphabet are your memory places, just as the pictures in Cicero's home were his memory places.

Say to yourself what's A? Apple should then spring to mind. Using the letter clues, most people will get eight items correct. Eight of ten—that's not bad. Furthermore, the serial position effect will not be present. That is, using the system, each item will have an equal probability of recall. Without using the system, the beginning and end of the list will have the highest probability of recall. Don't look. Tell me what's the G word? The H word? The F word? You should be able to recall the items in or out of order.

Use a Memory Frame to Recall Anything You Wish

I am trying to enlighten you on the advantages of using a memory peg list or memory frame on which to hang items you want to recall. Here is another example of the use of numbers as a peg list. At dinner parties, after people have fed to satiety and drunk a bit, there often arises a joke-telling session. Not to be left behind, I have memorized five jokes to tell on such occasions. Feel free, if you like, to use them at your next dinner party. Notice how a single word next to the number triggers the joke story and lets me look like a star. Here's the list:

1. Hearing
2. Horse
3. Willy
4. Saw
5. Priest

Here's how this list works for me: By the way, if the group doesn't get the joke, just step over it and go on to the next.

1. Hearing reminds me of the hearing aid joke. An old man notices sudden loss of hearing in his right ear. When his doctor looked in that

ear, he said, "What's this suppository doing in your ear?" The patient replied, "Doc, you solved two of my problems. Now I know where my hearing aid is."

2. Horse. John Major and the Queen were riding together in a horse-drawn carriage when the horse broke wind. John said, "I am so, so sorry, Your Majesty!" The Queen said, "That's all right, John, I thought it was the horse."

3. Willy (British slang for penis). "Darling, if you want sex, pull my willy once. If you don't want sex, pull my willy 76 times."

4. Saw. A customer bought a chainsaw because the salesman said it would cut down 250 trees a day. The first day it cut 250, but the second day only 230, and the third day only 210. So, the customer brought back the saw. "Let's have a look at this," said the salesman as he pulled the cord. And the customer said, "What's that noise?"

5. Priest. A Catholic priest from Dublin was walking on the west end of London when a young lady approached and asked, "How about a quickie, Governor? Five quid." Priest: "No thanks." Along the way, another woman asked, "Five quid for a quickie?" Priest: "No thanks." Farther down, a woman said, "Only five quid for a quickie." "No thanks." But the priest realized he didn't know what a quickie was and therefore didn't know what he was turning down. When he got back to Dublin, he called the convent next to the rectory and talked to the Mother Superior, "Sister, what's a quickie?" She replied, "Five quid. Same as London."

How About This?

Memorize and be prepared to recite the following letters in sequence. Take only 15 seconds for this task and write your answer: Llew derepmet reivalc. Now recognize the pattern and chunk it. Did you get the pattern? I don't blame you if you didn't. I didn't get it either when I first saw it. Hint: It is something familiar to most scholars of music.

This is "well-tempered clavier" with each word spelled backward. *The Well Tempered Clavier* is a collection of keyboard music by Johann Sebastian Bach. Now write the sequence by thinking of the key words and reading the words backward. You should have no trouble with llew (well spelled backward), but most people will have to break the second sequence into two parts dere and pmet because stage I of human memory can usually only hold seven items, not eight. Most people will be able to read the reivalc directly out of the memory by thinking of clavier backward; some will need to break clavier into two pieces and recall the rei and then the valc. The point is that it is easier to memorize something if you can chunk it, and it is easier to chunk it if you recognize a pattern.

The application of chunking to memorizing music is obvious. In music, the principal secret to rapid mastery of a given passage often consists in apprehending the designs. Take, for instance, the extended scale passage at the close of Chopin's Scherzo, Op.54. The scale begins at the lowest E and ascends to the highest. As soon as the rhythmic arrangement is observed, the entire passage can be played sans notes and without committing the latter to memory. It is now unnecessary to read every note; the experienced pianist sees at a glance that the scale of E is continued from the lowest to the highest E on a modern piano. These extreme points form the exterior lines which need to be memorized; anyone who properly understood this will produce an impression and thus obviate the seeming necessity for repeating the passage many times until it is "memorized." There is as little reason for reading every note in this passage as there is for spelling every word in the perusal of a soliloquy of *Hamlet* or spending two hours memorizing the letters of llew derepmet reivalc.

The Result of Chunking is Four-Fold Benefits:

1. You learn the piece faster.
2. The music acquired is better understood.
3. The material is more securely retained.
4. You get more time to have fun.
5. Because of 1-4, you will take your piano playing to a higher level.

For example, if you know that there is an organized sequence of chords in the standard blues piece, you can chunk that information—four measures of the tonic (I), two measures of subdominant (IV), two measures of the tonic (I), one measure of the dominant (V), one of the subdominant (IV), two measures of the tonic (I).

That chunking will give you a heads-up on memorizing the piece. This knowledge will help if the piece is in the standard sequence, which it usually is, and the knowledge will also help if it deviates from the standard by giving you a memory hook to recognize and encode the deviation. If you learn the formula for the standard chord progression, you will be able to play the blues in any key you learn, simply by applying the formula to that key.

But how to memorize the blues sequence itself? That's the question.

You have to work out your own system. As for me, I just say to myself 4-2-2 and picture going from C to F and back to C as an example. Check this out on the piano. Play a C chord four times, then an F chord two times, and then go back to the C chord twice. Nice sounds!

Then I tell myself a little story that after the two C's, we have to give G a chance if only for one measure, after which a jealous F (IV) jumps in for one measure before the I chord takes over again to finish things off twice. Telling myself the story a few times results in the encoding of the sequence so strong that I no longer need the mnemonics any more than a neurologist needs a mnemonic to remember the cranial nerves. After a while, you just know it. Even better is to chunk it to 422112 and play a few times to get the feel. The story helps you remember V-IV-I-I, but after a while, you won't need the story as a frame, and the 422112 will be enough to recall the blues sequence.

But what if you don't know what a tonic or a subdominant chord is? In that case, my friend, you can't chunk, and you are significantly behind the power curve. The best treatment for that situation is to correct your ignorance by doing significant work in your music theory book. Learn what those chords are and why they are called I, IV, and V. While you are at it, you may as well learn all the chords and the standard inversions of those chords, plus the arpeggios of those chords. Such knowledge will save you hours and hours of tedious memorization by giving you the chunking tools you need for fast encoding of the music in your memory. Hence, less time for work and more time for fun.

End of Part I

Whew! That was a lot of info about memory. So, let's take a breather. But before the breather and getting to Part II, the part that deals specifically with materials and methods, there is one more key general point about human memory that you should know about—motor memory, also known as kinesthetic memory, also known as muscle memory. I have also heard some people refer to this type of memory modality as finger memory. I saved the discussion of this aspect of memory for last because, in many ways, it is the most important since it does most of the work in any performance from memory. The trouble is that unconscious motor memory is unreliable, but is made less so by directing our attention to the way it works.

After your break and breather, come back and learn about the most powerful form of human memory and how it may be applied to memorizing Beethoven, Mozart, or any piece of music.

Pause here and take a break.

As for me, I will get a drink of water and check my email. Also, I will see if I recall that note sequence I made up. It started with C minor entering a bar. Come back when you are rested and ready to learn about motor memory. And you too, test yourself to see if the note sequence is or is not in your memory. How about the Blues Sequence? My bet is you recall the Blues Sequence better than the C minor entering the bar. The reason for that is the recency effect. Memory fades with time, and the Blues Sequence is more recent. Also, it is more important and more relevant to our goals than the C minor sequence, which probably relates to nothing relevant to your goals.

All Rested? Welcome Back!

Motor Memory, Kinesthetic Memory, Muscle Memory, and Finger Memory

O.K. We're back. Did you get the note sequence? If you didn't get the note sequence, go back and memorize the narrative and then proceed to the discussion of finger memory.

As for me, I tried but didn't quite get the note sequence correct. I forgot what to do with Eb when it left the bar. When I tried the sequence at the piano, the correct sequence was obvious. My experience confirms the importance of review to make sure that you have things correct and also shows the important way that playing the notes on the piano can cue the memory. Testing yourself is a way of cementing the memory. Did you get the Blues Sequence? How did you recall it? Can you play it starting with the C chord? If so, good for you.

Finger Memory

Fingers have no memory, of course. The memory is in the brain, without which the fingers cannot function. "Finger memory" is but a name for whatever the hands have been trained in advance to execute. The fingers may acquire a muscular habit of performing feats and evolutions, but the fingers have no memory. You can prove this by cutting the nerves to your fingers. The fingers will instantly become useless and will have no memory whatsoever. (Only kidding. For heaven's sake, please don't do that. Cutting the nerves to your fingers will result in disaster.)

Kinesthetic Motor Memory Is Hard to Beat

Motor memories are mainly non-verbal, non-visual memory programs stored initially in special regions of the brain (basal ganglia and cerebellum). The physical basis of these memories is well known to neuroscientists and consists initially of visual, tactile, auditory, and kinesthetic memories which, when over-learned, are then delocalized and stored diffusely throughout the brain in a kind of hologram. Because they are delocalized and stored diffusely, these over-learned motor memories are virtually indestructible. Thus, these motor memories are the best and most powerful memory encoding systems that we have. The human brain devotes trillions of bytes of storage capacity to these memories. Motor memory is what enables us to ride a bike long after our childhood experiences with biking. Motor memory also allows us to ride the bike without consciously thinking about the task. The motor program for bike riding has essentially become subconscious and non-verbal. Don't believe me? Try explaining to someone how to ride a bike. Try explaining it to yourself. See what I mean? It's not easy. It is much easier to get on the bike and ride away. We learn bike riding by doing. We teach bike riding by showing and then making the student ride.

No normal person has to use their intellect consciously to walk: we walk without mental effort. An effort of will is necessary to start walking, but it is the subconscious non-verbal habitual motor programs of the brain that keep us going. In fact, much of the brain's work is done automatically, including the maintenance of heart rate, blood pressure, and the chemical content of the blood. To be conscious of your breathing is to breathe irregularly: to be conscious of your walking is to walk—well, self-consciously. In the same way, we learn multiple tasks (driving, swimming, playing music) by repeatedly doing the tasks so that we can do them without conscious effort. That is, in fact, the effect we are seeking in our music performance, an effect we call AUTOMATICITY. Ultimately, we would like to play our pieces that way—automatically, without much conscious thought, just the way we ride our bikes without much conscious thought or the way we tie our shoelaces without thinking.

Warning! Motor Memory Can Betray You

As I am typing this book, I am not giving any conscious thought to what letter keys to press. I have typed 20 books and millions of words, so I don't need to think of what key to press. In fact, if I think about the keys, I will foul up. That's another point: Because motor memory is usually undirected by the intellect, it is traitorous. Consequently, in performance, a single wrong note may throw a player off, and they will break down (if they let themselves). Nor can they usually pick up the piece a bar or two farther on.

The good news is that the over-learned motor program is so deeply embedded in the brain that it functions automatically. The bad news is that the programs are such that they often fail if interrupted. That happens to me a lot. If you have had any recital experience yourself, I am sure it has happened to you also. Usually, the thing that interrupts me is my own thought about something other than the music task at hand. Even though the thought is just an idle moment, it sometimes has the power to derail the performance. Lately, I have been getting better at focusing attention on the performance and avoiding distracting thoughts. Consequently, my performances have been breaking down less often.

Because I have typed so many books, I don't have to think about typing any more than I have to think much about driving my car or flying my airplane. I hope someday my piano playing will be as automatic as flying and driving. If I keep at piano playing, it must happen that way, as that is the way my brain works, your brain works, our brains work. Sooner or later, you will be able to find and play the right keys on the piano without thinking much about them. Just keep working, and see.

Some Startling Examples of the Strengths of Motor Memory

Memo: The human brain is programmed to memorize motor sequences, and those sequences, once over-learned, cannot be easily destroyed.

Example: I have had demented patients who do not know their own name or where they are. When I place a bicycle in the hands of those patients, they tell me they don't know what the object I have placed in their hands is or what it does. And yet, those demented patients, without apparent effort, can get right on the bike and ride away. I have a demented patient who can play the piano quite well, including *Sidewalks of New York* and *Give My Regards to Broadway*. And yet, he is unable to tell what those songs are about, and he is unable to explain what or how he is playing. The motor memory is preserved even though the other memories (verbal, visual) are gone, long gone and, sadly, probably gone forever.

Why Is Motor Memory the Strongest Modality of Human Memory?

Motor memory systems probably evolved to enable humans to automatically manipulate weapons while consciously planning hunting strategies. Musicians can take advantage of the same motor memory capabilities of the brain by encoding their pieces not so much in verbal or visual modalities of memory, but in the motor memory itself. This might create psychological problems because you might not think you know a music piece. And let's face it, you probably don't know that piece—not consciously. And yet, you do know it—unconsciously. You know it in the non-verbal realm—the motor modality of human memory. A good treatment for that problem is to make sure you know how to begin your piece and the exact right note and beginning sequence to start. Once started in the right direction, motor memory should take over and keep going unless interrupted.

Aye, there's the rub. As every real pianist knows, if a motor sequence is interrupted, the program may fail. Don't believe it? While you are playing a piece you know by heart, have a friend turn on the radio. Or, while playing a piece, momentarily shift your consciousness to something else, even something silly like "Gee, I am playing this piece very well."

How true! In fact, congratulating myself on how well I am playing is the usual distraction that causes me to foul up.

The Story of Oscar Levant

Oscar Levant, one of the great pianists of all time and a friend of George Gershwin, stopped in the middle of *Rhapsody in Blue* while playing in Lewiston Stadium circa 1944. Levant had played *Rhapsody* many, many times. But this time, he momentarily thought of something else (according to him—his paycheck) and lost it.

What did Levant do? He didn't know how to continue, so he did an unusual thing: he and the orchestra started back at the beginning. And from that new beginning, Oscar kept going without apparent difficulty because he concentrated on the piece and didn't think about the paycheck until the performance was over. The whole instructive story of this event is featured in Levant's delightful autobiography, *Memoirs of an Amnesiac*.

Levant could have used some other tricks besides going back to the beginning. He could have asked himself not what was needed but where he had played the piece last. He could have then visualized the room and the piano where he practiced. As that image flashed across the slate of his consciousness, the forgotten item should have a high probability of being recalled. Cicero used this type of place clue during his speeches before the Roman Senate. The visual items that helped recall were always items in his own villa—a statue, a fresco, the impluvium, and so forth. Place clues (as they are called in the memory schools) helped Cicero recall what he wanted to talk about next. In fact, the word "topic" comes from the Greek work "topoi," which means—you guessed it—places. Next time you can't think of a name, think of a place where that name was learned. Thinking of the place and the events, sights, sounds, smells, tastes, emotional state, and any other thing at the time you previously played the piece should clue the memory.

Forgot where you left the house keys? Do not think of when you left them. Think of the last place you remember seeing them or using them. Place is a much more powerful memory clue than time. Review mentally your vacation experiences. You will be able to recall much more about the places you visited than you will be able to recall when you visited those places. In fact, you will have vivid memories of vacation locations that will far exceed in vividness any memory of what time you spent in those places and when. This is true for most humans: place memory is a thousand times better than time memory.

Remembrance of Things Past

Proust recalled his whole past life and wrote a seven-volume novel (*A La Recherche Du Temps Perdu*) based on the associations triggered by the taste of that Madeleine cookie after it was dipped in tea. Strictly speaking, this was an involuntary memory in which the taste of the Madeleine summoned forth images of his aunt's house and his happy childhood. The same mechanism can be used to voluntarily recall items temporarily out of the consciousness. Just think of items that are close to the needed item—close in either time or place or both, putting or trying to put the needed memory in context.

Right now, I don't know what I ate at the Hotel Roanoke last Friday. But if I visualize the Regency Room, the people at the table, and the seating arrangements, it might come back. Yes, it did come back, popped right into my consciousness without any great effort. Lamb chops.

So, if you get stuck, ask where, not what. Also, remember the state-dependent problem. If you are stuck, keep calm. The tenser you get, the worse your chance of recall. If putting the memory in context does not work, you might have to go back to the last place in the piece that you recall. Restarting is usually considered déclassé, but what can you do? Desperate people do desperate things. Or why not skip ahead to your rescue spot and play from there? That's what people do, and no one (except the teachers and the real music aficionados) seem to notice.

Discussion of Rescue Techniques

Instead of restarting, a better trick (as mentioned) might be to have a place forward in the piece that you can play. Call those places rescue spots because they really are lifesavers. If you are stuck, you don't go back, you don't repeat, you just skip ahead to the place you have already designated as your lifesaver. Few in the audience will notice. Most of the audience will be doing the time-honored thing that most audiences do—thinking of something else or daydreaming. Some, alas, will be sleeping.

Another possible way out of a mental block is to pause to think. While you are pausing and thinking, you might play some cadences—the I chord followed by the V or perhaps the I-IV-V. Chances are your teacher will know what you are doing, but the lay audience won't know, and even if they do know, chances are that they won't care. And even if they do care, so what. It won't be the end of the world.

Emotions, Positive and Negative—Good, Bad, and Ugly Encode Memories

Emotional significance often determines what we remember and what we choose to forget. Human memory works best when the thing we are trying to remember has a personal emotional significance for us.

Think back on your own life. You'll see that this is true. We remember what is emotionally important to us, and we tend to forget what is not emotionally important to us.

I recall my first sexual experience in great vivid detail. Yet, I can't recall what I had for lunch last Wednesday or even what color socks I have on right now. From which follows, that we are better off trying to memorize a musical piece that we connect with on an emotional level than a piece that we don't connect with. If you like fast jazzy pieces, it would be hard to memorize a slow, romantic piece and vice versa. For this reason, I advise against trying to memorize a piece you don't like. And I advise that you not bother with a piece that you actually hate. Drop, without regret, any piece that you honestly dislike. Drop without regret any piece that is beyond you technically.

Whew! That was a lot to learn about the facts of memory. In the next volume, we will apply what we learned to music tasks. The applications are more important than anything else because piano playing is primarily a performance art.

Before we get to Part II, review the summary list below on human memory principles. Review these several times until they are part of your memory repertoire. A good time to review is just before you hit the hay. Believe it or not, the brain will work on encoding the items while you sleep.

You will know that you know the principles when you can successfully explain what the principle is and how it applies to memory. Challenge yourself on these items. Ask yourself questions about them. Quiz yourself right now, for instance, on state-dependent learning. Give yourself time to think. Explain state-dependent learning to yourself. This is a pain and will seem pedantic, but it is the right thing to do if you wish to actually know a subject, any subject, well. You are testing yourself to see if you really know it. By the way, you should test yourself on your pieces and songs to prove you know them or to prove you don't. The piano demands a monumental sacrifice of time and energy. After all that suffering and deprivation during countless hours of practice, why not prove to yourself that you got it right?

Review Time Is Never Wasted

After you have given yourself your answers, go back to that section in this book and see how many items and examples you recalled and how many you missed. Imagine how you can apply the principle to memorizing music. Remember, there is a gigantic difference between thinking you know something and actually knowing it. Prove to yourself that you know this stuff. Make at least three intelligent points about each of the following topics. When you can, go on to Part II.

Summary of Memory Topics and Review

Consider the following questions and requests:
What general activities benefit the brain?
Explain why lost opportunities are opportunities lost.
How do we know that forgetting is the default mode of human memory?
How much of a perfectly memorized piece will be recalled in two weeks if there has been no interim review or rehearsal?
How does review time affect memory?
How do sickness and boredom affect memory?
Why do associations produce recall?
What associations are best?
What roles do active attention and active mental engagement play in memory?
Why is cramming not the best way of memorizing music?
What mechanisms control stage fright and how does stage fright affect memory?
What is meant by modality-specific memories?
Name the six modalities of human memory.
Which of the six modalities of human memory is the strongest?
Do emotions play a role in encoding memories?

Extra Credit:

Explain why neurologists think TV is bad for your brain.
Arrange the following activities in terms of what is best (number 1) and what is worst for the brain's health:

a. Thinking and doing
b. Doing
c. Thinking
d. Watching without thinking or doing.

Explain why a positive mental attitude is important.
Some psychologists call motor memory "procedural memory." Why?

Some psychologists call explicit memory "declarative memory." Why?

Extra Extra Credit

What is the best way to develop your sight-reading capacity? (Give yourself a big pat on the back if you immediately said to yourself: "The best way to develop sight-reading is to sight-read.")

More Extra Credit

Explain what happens when neurons fire together.
Why do we need to forget almost everything we experience?
What is the serial position effect and how does it influence music memory?
What techniques can be used to compensate for the serial position effect?
Why would knowing the historical perspectives help your performance attain the correct stylistic, musical, and technical result in performance?

PART II: MATERIALS AND METHODS

What follows are suggestions. Look them over, think about them, and try the ones you like. Some might work; some might not. Remember, one size doesn't fit all. Some techniques and ideas might work well on one task and not on another. Ditto vice-versa. Some techniques might work well for you but not your sister, and vice-versa. The point is that you need to remain flexible and adapt to the particular requirements of the particular project.

Piano

It is advisable if you wish to be a happy piano player that you have a real acoustic piano. Madge told me a keyboard just doesn't cut it and she insisted that I buy a real piano. She was right. A real piano makes all the difference.

Get Yourself a Good Piano

Every piano, upright or grand, long-owned or new, is a treasure chest, a magical box awaiting you to give forth its gifts to elevate and enrich your life and the lives of those around you. So—get yourself the best piano that you can afford and have it tuned by the best tuner you can find.

Tuner reminds me. What's the difference between a piano and a fish?

Answer: You can't tune a fish. Get it? (Tune a fish sounds like tuna fish.) Oh, well. I am sorry. I will try not to do this again.

Consult Experts

Since I know very little about pianos, I can give very little advice. But I can speak from my own experience and I hope those experiences will help you.

Know the Value of the Pianos You Are Dealing With

I inherited a Steinway D piano from Marjorie Washburn, one of my patients, who was an excellent pianist and worked at a nightclub playing. Marjorie's D was her pride and joy home piano and she kept it in excellent shape until she got sick with a stroke. After she got sick, the piano was neglected. The D was very large and my wife Ethel did not think it fit well in our living room. Also, I was still in the workforce, so I didn't have time to do much of anything but take care of patients.

My neighbor, Bob Lockavara, was interested in getting a piano for his daughter and asked if he could buy the Steinway D. Not knowing much about pianos, nor about the value of a Steinway D, I sold the piano to him for $5,000. Much to my regret, I subsequently learned my mistake. Steinway D pianos are now available at prices from $50,000 to $169,000.

Whew! Life is difficult. And life is especially difficult when you are stupid. On the other hand, another way of looking at it is that I inherited the Steinway D and paid nothing for it and therefore was ahead $5,000.

Bob spent over $55,000 on the repairs of the piano that I sold to him, but in the end, he was happy with the results. So was I. Now, like every real pianist, I dream of owning a concert grand, among which number some of the finest pianos made. Concert grands are a joy to play, and I play them wherever and whenever I can (usually at hotels and colleges that I visit). But concert grands (seven to nine feet long) are just too large for my home. So, I need a new home for my dream piano.

Beware of spinets, consoles, and old worn-out studio pianos and uprights, many of which are clunkers, but some of which are as good as baby grands—so much depends on the make, year, and so forth that you may wish to consult an expert before shelling out large amounts of money.

My second piano was a Steinway Baby Grand which I purchased from the Houston Grand Opera. It was a practice piano from a practice room and, according to the agent, had hardly ever been used. The purchase price was $26,000. This piano was a real gem and Madge and I loved it.

About eight years later, Dave, one of my friends, said he had found the ideal piano for me—a Sauter made in Germany. Since I already knew I knew very little about pianos, I hired an expert piano appraiser to examine the Sauter and tell me about it. The serial number enabled him to trace the exact history of the piano, when it was born, when it came to the United States, who owned it (Forsey), and what it might be worth. I then hired another appraiser on the internet who gave much the same opinion as expert number one.

The asking price was $54,000, but I would get a credit on the trade-in of the Steinway Baby Grand of $26,000. My advisors said the trade-in was reasonable and the Sauter was worth about $104,000 because it was in excellent shape and was made of a beautiful special kind of cherry wood. The Sauter is a real gem and my wife and I love it. It adds beauty to our living room and I play it every day I am home. Coda: For insurance, the Sauter was appraised at $105,000. Dave was rewarded with a bottle of Black Bush Irish whiskey.

My next three pianos were uprights. One for our beach home in Galveston, Texas, and one for the home where my granddaughters live in Dallas and one for the home of my other grandchildren in Nashville. Dave suggested I test drive some Essex pianos made in China on the

Pearl River, but designed by Steinway. I found three that were excellent and sent two to the grandkids and one to the beach house. The cost was $3,500 each, a bargain if you look at what they are worth now. Delivery to Dallas and Nashville cost $850 each and delivery to the beach was free except the men couldn't get the piano up the stairs because the hallway was too narrow. A machine was rented ($550) to lift the Essex onto the veranda and the men moved it from there to the living room where I play it every weekend. Dave was rewarded with a bottle of Jameson Irish whiskey.

Ugh! I can't resist. What's the difference between an upright and a grand piano? Answer: The grand makes a bigger plop when dropped off a cliff.

What About Keyboards?

Keyboards are fine in their way, but you must memorize on the real piano if you are to play back effectively in recital and festivals. If you can't afford a piano, see if you can use one at a local college or high school. Or try to rent one. Yes, as a last resort, you might practice music on a keyboard. If you do have to use a keyboard, make sure it comes as close to a real acoustic piano as possible, including pressure-sensitive keys spanning 7 1/3 octaves (88 keys). I have two keyboards, one for my study when I want to try a quick tune and the other for car travel. If I get to a hotel where there is no piano, I install the keyboard in our room. It has earphones so I can practice without disturbing the neighbors.

About Travel

Most luxury liners have pianos available for practice. Queen Mary 2 has the practice piano on the lowest deck next to the crew quarters. The ship's musicians use it to practice, so you have to make a reservation just as they do. Queen Victoria doesn't require a reservation, and neither does Windstar or the multiple other ships I have been on. On the Cunard ships, if you are grill class (Princess or Queen), you can play in the Queen's grill lounge most times. I have never encountered a serious objection from the staff or fellow travelers there, but I always ask people in advance if they are OK with my practicing. And I have obtained permission from the grill concierge to play. With concierge permission, I can always overcome any objection.

Hotels

Most hotels have at least one piano, but some motels have none. With the hotels, the problem is finding where the piano is and then playing it. If you ask at the front desk, the usual response is either "we have no piano" or "guests are not permitted to play the piano." How to get around these two statements is a test of your creativity. For what it is worth, I will tell you about some of my experiences in the hopes my experiences might give you ideas.

"We have no piano." Often the desk person doesn't know if the hotel has a piano or not, so they give that routine answer. Housekeeping usually knows where the pianos are located. I have had the front desk tell me there is no piano and have had the housekeeper tell me, without reservation or hesitation, that the piano is in the basement or the attic. And yes, housekeeping has always been right. For instance, the Istanbul Hilton had a nice upright in a dark cluttered attic. There was no electric light that I could find, but I have a miner's light that attaches to my forehead that lights the music sheet nicely. I have spent happy hours in that attic playing without interruption. The basements are usually cluttered and not visited, so I have spent happy times in deserted hotel basements playing. Amazingly, basement and attic pianos have been in good condition. Once I was discovered at the Four Seasons Hotel Istanbul playing a Steinway Grand in the basement. The guard asked my room number and nodded after I gave it. That night I played at cocktail hour—just sat down and played. No permission asked. After about a half hour of playing American favorites, I took a break and Ethel and I were given martinis and bar food. The manager said, "pack your stuff. We are moving you and your wife to the presidential suite at no cost." That was a nice reward. The presidential suite occupied almost a whole floor and had a bathtub the size of a small swimming pool, a kitchen, several bedrooms, a fully equipped bar, an exercise room and so forth. We stayed three nights and thanked our lucky stars.

At the Arlington Hotel in Hot Springs, I have stopped asking about pianos because I know there is a Mason & Hamlin in ballroom B and I know how to turn on the lights. I have played that piano many times and have never been interrupted. Ballrooms at hotels have a 50% chance of having a piano. If the hotel has three ballrooms, there will be a 7/8 chance of finding a piano in one of the rooms.

"Guests may not play the piano." That is usually a routine answer if the hotel has a piano in full view. When I ask why guests can't play, the usual answer is "it's not permitted," which statement doesn't explain why, it just restates the rule. In logic, we call that a tautology, saying the same thing twice like "imports come from foreign countries" or "the undecided voters could go either way."

At the Old Mill Hotel in Toronto, in an empty ballroom, an old woman yelled at me when I sat down and played despite her telling me not to play. I tried to explain that it would not hurt the piano and might help keep the strings from rusting. "I work here and I am on duty. No! I asked you not to play. Please don't." The next day the same scene repeated with her screaming at me not to play. The next day a young woman was on duty. "Of course, play. I will be delighted." And I did my repertoire to her amusement. The lesson here is persistence counts.

Different countries seem to have different traditions. Wherever we went in Poland, I played in the main lounge in the afternoons and at cocktail hour and was never stopped and was always encouraged. Of course, in Poland, I only played Chopin pieces and no one there would ever interrupt or stop a Chopin. Chopin is a Polish national hero. Warsaw even has the airport and a vodka named after him. Japan was just the opposite. They never let me play and always stopped me if I started. In Japan, I usually got around this problem by asking the concierge where the nearest studio was. It was always within walking distance and the reception there was very polite. But I had to pay $30 an hour. Ireland is just the opposite. When I arrived in Dublin, I called the music department of Trinity College. They gave me the key to the practice hall and I played there in the afternoons and nights and weekends and weekdays. No one was ever there except a secretary in an adjacent office. Trinity College has a fine collection of pianos and harpsichords which I enjoyed. There was no charge whatsoever. When I asked the secretary if there were charges, she smiled, "Of course not. We're Irish."

What About Digital Pianos?

Acoustic or digital? That is the question. Let's use Aristotle's criteria of compare and contrast by looking at similarities and differences: A = Acoustic D = Digital

Sound Production

A makes sound by having hammers hit strings. D makes sound by electronics. In D, sounds that have been collected with excellent equipment are stored in the piano's memory. When you press a key, sensors detect how fast and hard your strike was and D produces the correct volume of sound. Thus, if you go D, a full-sized D with weighted keys is best. However, most people agree A makes a better sound. A gives a sound with more nuance and depth, and A responds with more sensitivity to the touch of fingers, speed of the stroke, and weight of the arms. D never needs tuning. A usually needs tuning twice a year with ordinary use and more often if used a lot. If it is hot in the house, A tends to go flatter; D doesn't change. If it is colder in the house, A tends to go sharper; D does not change. This is a very interesting phenomenon and most pianists have noticed that their A piano sounds different in the morning compared to the evening and different in winter than in summer. D does not change morning, noon, or night, summer, fall, winter, or spring.

Size

D fits into small spaces. D takes less space than a grand A and most D are not as tall as an upright A. Therefore, D is easier to move. You could even take your D to college. With D, you can plug in headphones and you won't annoy your family when you practice. You might even focus better when you don't hear noises from the TV in the next room. But when the power fails, as it sometimes does in Texas and sometimes fails for a week, D will not work and A will.

Sorry

All the digitals I have tried, including Spiro, do not have the feel or sound of a real piano. These machines, in my opinion, are not perfected yet.

Take Care of Your Piano and It Will Take Care of You

Once you have a good piano, take care of it. If something is wrong, have it fixed. Do not try to tune, repair, or clean the inside of your piano yourself. In general, do not let someone else clean the outside of the piano. Clean it yourself. If your piano tuner suggests, after he/she has tuned your piano, that your piano needs work, you will be well-advised to have that work done. Sometimes the work required is expensive and you may be better off buying another instrument. Ask your tuner for an estimate and decide accordingly.

That ends the materials section of Part II. The piano is one of the material things needed. The other material needed is yourself, a person to play the piano. Some of these items have been covered, some not. Let's see what's what.

The Big Five

You need training and a teacher and lots of work and practice to be a successful amateur pianist. Playing from memory is the desired effect.

The main means to memorize and perform music are five in number, the big five associative techniques:

Emotional association
Motor association
Aural association
Visual association
Intellectual (also known as conscious) association.

These items, which we call the big five, may be studied separately or together. They work best when closely coordinated so as to make music secure from even momentary failure. It is only in theory that we can divide these modalities into categories. In practice, all performance modalities mix together and work together.

Don't Be an Ordinary Piano Player

The ordinary piano player (as opposed to the pianist), who does not take his work seriously and has made no logical effort to train musical memory, employs, consciously and unconsciously, only motor memory and perhaps some ear memory when a piece is to go to memory. The ordinary piano player does not realize or does not care to know that he may possess several other means of developing his music. That is regrettable because a logical development of all faculties will quickly bring about astonishing results.

About General Health

Optimal performance on the piano has a better chance of happening when both physical and mental health are optimal. If you are sick, forget about memorizing music unless you must. Wait until you are well when things will go much better. If you are tired, rest before you start your practice session. Things will go much better.

In my view, there is no better hobby than music. In my prejudiced view, there is no better music hobby than playing the piano. But keep this hobby under control. Always rule your hobby and never let it rule you. Preoccupation with the piano should be temperate, intelligently controlled, and balanced in relation to the other things in your life.

It isn't my job to tell you to obtain regular exercise, put out those cigarettes, eat fruits and vegetables, socialize with others your age, get a good night's sleep, maintain a happy, upbeat, optimistic outlook on life, and so forth. You know what's good for your health and you know what isn't so good. So, let's skip the health, nutrition, and medical stuff and get down to the business of making music.

Practical Strategies to Enhance Music Performance

The strategies in this part divide themselves, again like ancient Gaul, into three parts:

1. Organization
2. Effective Practice Behavior
3. Mnemonic Tricks Related to the Use of the Big Five Associative Techniques

1. Organization—Get Organized

A lot depends on your becoming organized in your approach to music because organization is so important to good piano playing.

Yes, friends, organization is fundamental to developing and maintaining a good performance. You need to create effective systematic routines for handling your music tasks. Some organizational strategies can be created quickly and easily and simply. Other strategies are hard because they require some investment in time, energy, thought, and sometimes money. Being organized is a matter of creating an effective system to handle the everyday situations that require music memory and performance. Once your system is in place and running smoothly, you can deploy your mental energy for more creative, productive, and gratifying purposes. Your first task in getting organized is to get yourself an instrument that you like and that likes you, as discussed above.

Organize Your Practice Environment

Get control of the practice environment. Tell friends and family to leave you alone when you are trying to practice and especially when you are trying to memorize your piece. Leaving you alone means no interruptions. And you must discipline yourself to leave them alone and not be distracted by all the things that can distract us these days. Discuss this with the members of your household and try to reach a schedule for practice that will ensure that you get quality time for practice. The ideal situation is to have a soundproof music room where you practice and play. But most houses do not have such a room. The piano is usually set up in the living room with the pianist's right side, not back, open to the room.

Never ever compromise your art and your love for music by letting other people control your practice. Never feel that your practice in any way is having an adverse effect on the others in the home. If the noise bothers them, they can leave or they can put on the ear protectors that people use at shooting ranges to block out sounds. These muffs are extremely effective. Make sure there is no noise in the practice room—that means no clocks that tick, radios that blast, TVs that shout. No nothing that makes noise or can make noise.

Never ever cater to what you think are the needs of others by playing too softly or anything but correct notes. In general, playing loud will make a bigger impression on your brain and motor memory than playing softly. Besides, you are the artist! Act like one. What we are talking about is developing you as an artist for your lifetime. To do that, you must learn. You must practice. Remember, Beethoven stopped in the middle of a piece and walked out of a drawing room because some Duke talked to his wife during the performance. Music is that important! Recently, Hans Graf (Houston conductor) stopped a performance because of a ringing cell phone in the audience! He continued after the silence.

The serious student of the piano, no less than the soldier, must be subject to iron discipline. The development of the muscles of the human body requires systematic exercise, and much hard work over a long time. That's a fact that you must learn to live with and adjust to. Surely there is no need to tell you that you need muscle power to play your instrument and you need speed, agility, accuracy, and endurance, all of which need development through practice.

It Is Hard to Avoid Distractions, But You Must

How did we get in this mess?

Why are there so many distractions?

Advances in technology play a big part, pooling information, disseminating it easily, and offering the means to interrupt nearly every task before it is finished. This is an alteration of the traditional rhythms of life, giving us more things to pay attention to and thinner slices of time to devote to each one. Don't let that happen to your music time. "Information overload," a term coined by Alvin Toffler in 1970, is now a chronic condition of modern life. Fight back. Yes, you need to fight back. And for good reasons.

Music Requires Focused Attention

Memorizing music and music performance is a full concentration, one focused job that just doesn't fit in with multitasking. You might be able to talk on your cell phone at the same time as you drive your car or ride your bike, but you can't memorize your music while talking on the phone. Don't believe me? Try it.

Although conscious attention can be given only to one thing at a time and concentrated attention is needed to memorize your piece, it is a fact that the subconscious mind can direct multiple operations simultaneously (else how could we breathe, digest food, pump our blood all at once).

Without the intervention of the subconscious motor memory systems, our music performances would be limited in scope and character. The magic in performance is in the mix of conscious and subconscious control. But for the initial stage of actually memorizing, conscious attention to the task is the ticket. Your conscious mind must be the director of your memory task. It must select the material. It must train habits. It must criticize work done. Your conscious mind must correct mistakes. And it must put the piece into memory. Consciousness, of which man is rightly proud, is but a small area of his mind. Behind it is the vastly older and more comprehensive mind, subconscious and automatic (and, sadly, somewhat reptilian), which can be occasionally trusted to play its part automatically when the time comes.

Repeat After Us: Music Requires Undivided Attention

Our brains evolved in a far simpler environment. Like a Model T Ford at the Indianapolis Speedway, they poke along, doing what they can, but they have trouble keeping up at the current speeds. In brief, scientists have discovered that there are distinct limits to what our brains can do and distinct limits on what we can do to improve functioning. When a task is complex and involves anything other than managing what scientists call simple information or trivial tasks, full concentration without interruption is needed. Because your understanding of this important point is so necessary, we will give some reasons that you must ensure your music memory task time is fully protected from interruption.

Why Interruption Is Bad

Working memory is fugitive because (as discussed) it is encoded in the electrical activity of brain cells. As we try to remember a new phone number, neurons in our frontal and parietal lobes are firing away. By contrast, the long-term memory or where we parked our car is encoded in the strength and topography of connections between neurons in the brain as a whole and particularly in the temporal lobes. Attention works the same way: Neurons increase their activity as we concentrate on an object or task, and they slow their firing when something else intervenes. It is true that the brain can accomplish many things at once (for instance, drink coffee and read the newspaper), but it can only pay careful attention to one thing at a time. This concentrated form of attention is so precious that it is easily depleted. To summarize this important point:

There is a mismatch between our modern lives and our anciently evolved brains that is most evident in the problems of working memory and attention in complex tasks like memorizing music.

But there is another culprit.

Our Brains Overvalue the New and the Now

We are easily distracted because we overvalue what happens to us now compared to what comes in the future. This attention to now was, of course, a major survival technique when the saber-toothed tiger was at the cave. You addressed that problem now, or you got eaten (and if you got eaten you weren't around to worry about anything else—end of story).

Furthermore, as discussed, the human brain likes and pays attention to novelty. Thus, interruptions take advantage of the brain's natural bias toward paying attention to something different and new. The biases of attention to now and the attention to new served well in our species' evolutionary past when the future was uncertain and the now could well be a threat that deserved immediate attention. Nowadays, the new is more often trivial than essential. Learn to pay less attention to modern distractions and more attention to the task.

Organize Your Body to Play

Part of getting organized involves the way you sit and position yourself and your hands. Correct position and posture will affect how well you play and how easily. Your back should be straight. You should lean slightly forward toward the piano. Shoulders should be relaxed, and forearms and hands should make a straight horizontal line when your fingertips are resting on the keys. Try to feel comfortable and relaxed whenever you sit at the piano. Adjust the seat to the height and the distance that makes you feel most comfortable; usually, you should be able to reach the fallboard with your fists. Arms should be level (say some books) as you place fingers on the keys. Many people sit too high over the keys and this can cause tension. Find out what is most comfortable for you and use that position.

Reality Check

Sit down and start to work on your piece. Usually, within minutes of starting practice, you will be interrupted by some other task. Shut that task off and make sure it stays off. Turn the TV off. Shut down the computer. Check in with your Facebook friends later. They can wait. Do not answer the telephone. If the interruption is caused by a person, explain firmly but politely that you need private, uninterrupted time to work on memorizing a piece by Beethoven or whomever. Not only will they be impressed, but they will also defer.

Effective Practice Behavior

This book is about having fun memorizing your pieces and not about how to practice. We will soon come to specific information on music memory. Meanwhile, I can't forbear giving some advice about practice behavior.

Practice Every Day

Practice every day for one hour. If you like, record in a book the exact time you start practice and the exact time you finish. Write down what you did, which pieces were played, what scales, and so forth. If you don't actually practice for an hour, make up the additional time on the following day. If you miss the hour of practice entirely, then do two hours the next day.

Following this discipline has improved my playing. And my time at the piano has become a delight. However, my program of discipline doesn't stop there. Each Sunday I review and play from memory my entire repertoire. During the week, if after my hour of practice is over and I have spare time, I play pieces I like for fun and I practice sight-reading. For me, fun is important. How about you?

Remember the distributive rule? Regular daily practice is far better than playing for several hours once or twice a week. A little practice a lot of times works much better than a lot of practice done in a single block of time. Frequent repetitions (often ad hoc) at intervals are much much better than frequent repetitions at one enduring block of time. Obey the distributive rule: Space the repetitions. Do not cram.

How Long Will It Take Before You Become an Expert at the Piano?

The usual reply to that question is "much longer than you think." That reply, of course, begs the question. A more realistic answer would be, "A long, long time." Yes, friends, the sad news from recent research is that to master any complex discipline one needs at least 10,000 hours of study. This 10,000-hour rule applies across the board whether you want to be a great neurosurgeon, an effective lawyer, a prize-winning scientist, an Olympic athlete, or a great pianist. Do you have any doubt that Mozart, Liszt, Beethoven, MacDowell, men of that ilk, spent more than 10,000 hours on their work? Is there any neurosurgeon in the world who has not spent more than 10,000 hours learning how to practice medicine? The point is that if your goal is real achievement at the piano, or at anything else worthwhile, much time and effort will be required, much more than people think. Much more than you think.

Bottom Line

Conclusion: The more you play and the more often you play, the better you will become. But try to spare the folks at home by practicing alone or on your own while others are not around. In the early days of my piano career, I usually saved the scales and cadences for the times that my wife was out of the house. When she was home, I tried to concentrate on the pieces. These days I don't do scales and I don't do cadences. Instead, I concentrate on pieces. They are much more fun and my wife doesn't mind them.

Moderation in All Things

Don't be a harmless drudge. There is no virtue in practicing eight hours a day. Conscious work is fatiguing to the brain. Professional musicians may have to put in extra hours occasionally, but I believe no one should practice more than three or four hours a day. One hour a day is probably best for amateurs, and that hour is probably best divided into four 15-minute segments. It doesn't take long to repeat a passage two or three times (usually only ten minutes). During that time before brain fatigue sets in, you can focus critical attention on predetermined aspects of the music. Short periods of attention are best. Your thoughts will not wander and work will be done well. Balance out your life with other fun activities.

The best musicians (and the best teachers of music) I believe, like the best artists and writers, are well-rounded with a large knowledge of human nature, culture, history, and a vast experience with life in general.

Progress Will Be Slow

Be patient. Progress will be slow, much slower than most people imagine. Be easy on yourself too. Perfection is rarely achieved in this wide world, but it is a reasonable goal to work toward. Try to learn something new every day. Play your pieces slowly and carefully at first, and then when you can play correctly and evenly, gradually work up to the composer's tempo. When you can play the piece five times in a row correctly, congratulate yourself, for it is probable that you actually know it at the moment. But everybody's memory fades, even yours. So be prepared to have to refresh your memory when it needs refreshing.

Metronome practice might give you a good idea of what the correct tempo might be. If the metronome helps, use it. If the metronome doesn't help, don't use it. Usually, the metronome makes me feel bad because I usually can't measure up to the proper tempo and it sounds too mechanical. But I can solve that problem by turning it down to some speed that I can do and still have the music sound good. After I have mastered the piece at slow tempo, I can usually gradually increase speed until I get where I want to go. Once I am at tempo, then I can start to add personal touches to bring energy, interest, and spontaneity to the performance, trying to make the most beautiful sounds that I can, bringing the music alive. So, if you are like me, you will start slow and gradually get faster, and then, after you are at the speed that is right, you will put in your artistic embellishments.

Final word about fast tempi: The only thing that slows me down is lack of speed.

Doctor Ethel Patten (Student Patten's wife): That was a (half-baked) joke, of course. Lack of speed and slowing down are two ways of saying the same thing. Furthermore, that can't be the only thing that slows him down. He's slow because he's an old man.

Play Every Piano You Can

Use every opportunity to play every piano you can. Those of you who have had some experience know that no two pianos sound the same or have the same response to finger pressure.

In fact, due to variations in temperature, humidity, and God knows what, my baby grand Steinway piano does not sound the same in the morning as it does at night. But my Sauter grand piano does seem to sound the same regardless of the time of day. Go figure.

Why Play Different Pianos

It helps to get familiar with the wide range of feel of strange keyboards on strange pianos. Get familiar with the wide range of heights of strange piano stools. Get as wide an experience as you can with the variations intrinsic to your instrument and to the variations intrinsic to pianos in general. It pays to get familiar with all the different pianos that you might have to play during festivals and recitals and at hotels during cocktails. Eventually, you will know what to expect from a Steinway versus a Baldwin versus a Young Chang versus a Kawai versus a Sauter, Kimball, William Knabe, Mason & Hamlin, Schomer, Wurlitzer, Bergmann, Howard (may the gods help us!), and the rest.

Once you have a repertoire firmly in memory, it doesn't hurt to play it on these pianos under different circumstances, even with external noise and distractions. Real-life musicians have to learn to deal with sneezes, plates dropping, impolite people talking to their stock broker, cocktail chatter, and so forth. All that comes with the territory during recital in informal conditions. If you are used to it, you will do better. If you are not used to it, you may flub.

How to Get to Play Other People's Pianos

My method, one of my methods anyway, is to ask at hotels where we are staying if I can play in the ballroom on the concert grand. Most times the ballroom is not in use and the hotel management is eager to help me find a piano to play. But be warned, most hotel clerks know little. Recently at the Hilton in London I asked at the desk if there was a piano in the hotel. "We used to have one, but it was sold." Two minutes later, I asked the concierge at the same hotel the same question. "We have a piano, but it is in storage." Three minutes after that I asked the event planner for the same hotel. "Our piano is a wreck and was withdrawn from service and is now in storage and unavailable for you to play." Fifteen minutes later, I asked at the business center and the woman there suggested I talk to housekeeping. Four minutes after that I talked with the woman in charge of housekeeping. Bingo! Mrs. Housekeeping showed me to the Yamaha in a deserted room. She said I could play as much as I wanted from five o'clock to eight the next morning.

Another Hotel Trick

It's gutsy, but I have played at cocktail hours around the world and at fancy restaurants. The musical standards out there are quite low. The usual reception, both on the part of the patrons and management, to my (at this point pretty poor playing) is wonderful. Free drinks and food have been offered at bars and restaurants as an inducement to play on. My best reward so far was at The Four Seasons Hotel in Istanbul upgrading our room to the Presidential Suite. I have never been refused the use of the piano on cruise ships. Talk with the ship's musician and get permission to tickle the ivory. Some cruise ship pianos are locked. The musician has the key, usually in his shirt pocket just above his heart.

Play before these ad hoc audiences and any other people who will listen. The experience is invaluable because the experience of initial nerves will help you overcome recital jitters and get you used to playing before an audience. Lesson: The more you play, the easier it gets.

Don't Bite Off More Than You Can Chew

In playing for ad hoc audiences, avoid vagueness. Know what you want to play and how you want to play it. Play cold, without a warm-up. And certainly, don't play Hannon or scales for 15 minutes. Remember: Keep going even if there are mistakes and blackouts. Don't stop and don't back up. Do think ahead, for thinking ahead often helps avoid flubs. But don't think too far ahead, for that often can cause flubs.

If you are uncertain about a given piece, consult your teacher or other qualified person. Clear up everything that lacks precision before you play before a group of strangers. Another menace: Try to understand the limits imposed on you by nature and by your present level of skill. Don't undertake to play a piece that is not well within your performance level. That is a common human failing. We are ambitious and want to outdo ourselves. And we are not alone: Comedians want to play tragedy. The old man wants to be a young premier. The simple type longs for heroic parts. The soubrette for the dramatic. Don't follow their errors! Be yourself! Know your limits! Drop, without regret, any piece that you find is beyond you technically.

Be Prepared for Rejection

Expect to be turned down sometimes. Rejection is a normal part of life; don't take a rejection seriously. Try to find out the reason that they don't want you to play their piano. You might be able to work around that reason. At Monte Grotto Terme, Italy, the front desk clerk at the Garden Hotel wouldn't let me play between 1:00 and 4:00 PM because most of the German tourists were taking naps at that time. So, at that hotel, I played after 4:00. The Sheraton Hotel in Addis Ababa, Ethiopia, gave me the runaround by telling me no one had the key to the piano. The next day the story had changed to only the pianist can play. Other excuses that I have gotten include, "That is not a real piano. It is fake and placed in the lobby only for show." "The piano is played only on special occasions." "Guests are not allowed to play." After this last reply, I asked why guests are not allowed to play. The answer came back: "Because that's the rule." When I said that I had asked the reason for the rule and not a restatement of the rule, the desk clerk shouted, "No!"

Select Your Music Carefully

In general, choose music which you know well and which you can play without hesitation and from memory. Do not play the most complicated pieces that you know, or the most recent that you have studied. Out of respect for your audience, vary the program. Pick tunes with different rhythms, speeds, and tempos.

That's good advice. I alternate classical pieces with pop so my playing does not all sound the same.

Vary the dynamics (soft and loud in the same piece promotes interest, and the music usually begins and ends softly with the louder parts in between). Save your best for last, as that is what they are most likely to remember and that is what they will most likely use to appraise your overall performance.

Nursing Homes, Retirement Homes, and Assisted Living Facilities Need Pianists

Our tap group does tap shows at local nursing homes, senior centers, and assisted living facilities. Usually, I arrive early, find the piano, and start playing. Within minutes I am surrounded by an attentive and appreciative crowd of old folks. With this audience, the problem has been breaking away. They want the music to play on and on and on. Some nursing home inmates are so lonely, they will try to physically keep you at the piano playing for them. The situations at the homes for demented people are even more pathetic. They want and need someone to pay attention to them and to help them recall the good old songs of bygone days. When I explain I have to leave, they cry.

Performance in Informal Settings Goes Better If You Look at Ease and Confident

But this above all—look confident! Smile as much as possible. Have an open body posture and give your audience some direct eye contact. Your audience likes to see happy people and likes to feel that they are in direct personal contact with a real human being. In some settings, it is proper to bow before you start and announce your piece. The bow acknowledges the grand introduction that the master of ceremonies gave to you. Then play your piece, coloring your piece your color. Audiences love the individual artist who doesn't play like a machine. Our society needs more of the human touch to neutralize the high-tech environment that we live in.

Keep Your Mouth Shut

Let the playing speak for itself. Keep your comments to a minimum. Never say stupid things like, "Jesus, I need more practice" or announce that you can't play well. That is the kiss of death because this kind of talk will prejudice the audience against you. And it may also trip you up by becoming a self-fulfilling prophecy. In law, testimony contrary to interest is considered extremely valid. Say something against yourself and the judge and jury will tend to believe you. In our social lives, if you say something against yourself, the audience is likely to believe it because speaking against self-interest would be considered quite unusual.

Summary of Advice

Never say anything against yourself for two reasons:

1. Others may believe it.
2. You may believe it.

HOW TO HANDLE MISTAKES

❖ ❖ ❖

When you make a mistake (notice we said "when" you make a mistake, not "if" you make a mistake), do not call attention to it by shaking your head, biting your lips, apologizing to the audience, or going back to correct the wrong notes. Just keep going. Most audiences most of the time are not paying much attention to you or your playing, especially at hotel cocktail hours where most of the people in your audience are, or will soon be, half wasted.

Are Wrong Notes Really Sinful?

Some teachers think that a pianist must be a scholar. They believe that this is an age where the document rules, the score is sacrosanct, and the urtext is supreme. These teachers sit in judgment, the music in hand, peering at each marking. If the student dares to overlook a staccato, he or she is considered inept, a defiler of the composer's intention. And of course, in this context, wrong notes are considered sins.

All that strikes me as pretty funny. The indefatigable pursuit of an unattainable and often unavailing perfection is a waste of time and talent. In a competition today, an Anton Rubinstein or de Pachmann would be thrown out in the first round. Did Liszt play all and only the right notes in his *Transcendental Etudes*? How many slips did he have? Nobody knows and nobody cares. My recent experience in competitions indicates there might be a loosening up of the "standardized" performance, and a flight of imagination or a creative rendition is not as suspect as it was before. In one competition at San Jacinto Junior College, a young lady (about 13 years old) got lost in Debussy's *Reverie* and played one of the five parts twice and omitted part four (the part that starts in E major). Nevertheless, she received honors for her performance and she deserved it because she had entered the spirit of the piece, creating beauty and a daydream atmosphere and tonal character that was a unique interpretation—hers.

PIANO BY HEART

Best Advice

If you flub, keep the rhythm and the pulse of the music right on. Rhythm and pulse, that's the ticket, the winning ticket. Most audiences will not notice wrong notes, but they will detect an alteration of rhythm or tempo. Here's the rule: Wrong notes? Forget it and keep on playing in the same style and rhythm. Your audience will be happy as clams.

Second Best Advice

Always know what key you are playing in and the cadences for that key. If you are really stuck, play the cadences and go on to the part of the piece you can play. If need be, play the cadences several times as a kind of vamp until your mind gets back into the groove of the piece.

Recently, I attended a fashion show with my granddaughters, Arden and Miranova. The fashion models were wonderful and waved to us each time they walked the aisle. But the piano player was not wonderful. He was just banging out cadences, and those were not even in sync with the fashion models. We were standing next to the piano, so I was there when the Master of Ceremonies came over and told the pianist that his services were no longer required. Yes! He was fired on the spot and deserved it. Moral of the story: Sometimes cadences can be annoying. Don't overdo them.

From Time to Time Record Your Performances

Making a video of your playing is fun and instructive. My Sony camera cost very little. It has a button that will delay the start of the movie for about eight seconds, giving me time to get into position to play. Reviewing your own performances can be a sobering experience. My first reaction was shock because the piece I thought I had played so well sounded not so good. There were places where I sped up (the easy parts) and places where I slowed and hesitated (the harder parts). My stage presence was awful. My posture ditto. At least I got to see and hear what was wrong. Without knowing what needs improvement, it is hard to improve. I hope you have the same experience: After years of playing, I saw that I was actually making mistakes for which I would likely find fault in anyone else. I could hardly believe my ears, and yet the unrelenting video machine showed in some places I had failed to play both hands together and had paused at the bar lines. On the other hand, I did notice that I had brought out nuances, emphasized different voices, and employed special accents that made the music much more musical. Next time, I shall attempt to accentuate the positive and eliminate the negative. My real criterion for success is (and please don't laugh): Did I play better than a machine? I set my goals low, real low, so I am not disappointed. If you set your goals low, you won't be disappointed either.

Save Some of Your Videos to Evaluate Your Progress or Lack of Progress

The video camera marks the date and time of the performance. Save some of your videos. When you review them a few weeks later, compare what happened then with what is happening now. You will probably be satisfied that you are in fact making progress. Advanced memory students also use the video to construct a mental movie of themselves playing the piece. This is the story or narrative technique that we have discussed, only applied this time to the visual modality with the additional benefit of having movement to facilitate recall by looking at the video. Videos of your hands playing are particularly interesting, and if you turn off the sound, the hands look as if they are dancing on the keyboard while very excited (and if we didn't know better) they actually look like they are having fun.

Select the Piece for Memory

Consult with your teacher and decide with the teacher what piece might be next. Never try to memorize something you don't like. Debussy puts me to sleep, so I know I would have difficulty memorizing *Reverie*. Rachmaninoff wakes me up, so I know I would relish memorizing *Prelude Opus 3, Number 2 in C-Sharp Minor*, which starts as you recall "Boom! Boom! Boom!"

Never try to memorize a piece way above your technical level. Always assure yourself that not only can you memorize the selected piece, but you will memorize it. Do not assume that memorizing the piece is or will be a prodigious feat. It won't be. It will be a normal part of your progressive musical career. Keep calm. This is music memory, not brain surgery.

Feelings Count

Your feelings are important when it comes to memory. If you connect with a piece on an emotional level, it will be easier to memorize. Beware of arrangements. There are lots of arrangements out there, some good, some bad, and some ugly. Your teacher will tell you whether or not the arrangement is okay for performance at festivals or recitals. In general, it is better to memorize the original music by the original composer than to deal with some simple and simplistic and often second-rate arrangement. Also, although it may sound strange for you to learn that, given the way the tonal system in the Western world is constructed (each scale is the same in pitch sequence change), some pieces in my opinion definitely sound better in the key in which they were originally written. Some sound much better. This is particularly true for popular music, which is definitely better in the original key.

In general, it is better to select a piece yourself that you like than to be stuck with a piece that someone else (like the teacher) has selected for you. When looking for new pieces to memorize, let your teacher review several with you so that you have some say-so in what piece you are going to work on.

Rote Memory is a Waste of Time and Energy

Make up your mind that you are not going to memorize your piece by rote. No, not you. By rote, I mean in a mechanical manner, by routine, especially by the mere exercise of memory without proper understanding of or reflection upon the music.

Say no to rote! Especially say no to note-by-note rote!

You are going to use memory science to organize your approach and to help you memorize the piece in the shortest, most efficient manner. With the application of science, concentration may be induced by interest, time saved by intelligent planning, and nervous strain avoided by knowledge of the neuroscientific laws that control human memory.

Before You Start to Memorize, Make Sure You Can Play the Piece Fairly Well from Notes

Go over the piece with your teacher. Iron out the difficulties and make sure you understand the piece and play it correctly from notes before you attempt to do any memory work. The major innovation that promoted memory of music was the written score. Make sure you have that in hand to study and that you understand it as best you can. Analysis of the written score will be an important tool to help you memorize your music.

Artist-teacher Anton Nel, in an interview published in *Clavier Companion* (March/April 2011) said, "I absolutely do not recommend muscle memory alone: while the fingers do know where to go after a certain number of repetitions, I find this method alone is unreliable. I study music away from the keyboard a lot (on planes, on the treadmill at the gym), making sure that I know the structure, harmony, left hand alone, and voice leading (especially in more contrapuntal music)." Bravo! The score is his friend (and your friend), and for him rote memory is not his method nor a good method of memorizing music.

What sometimes works for me is to copy the score and study it in detail, marking up the parts and assigning names or letters or both to the parts for easy reference. Some people will even mark the chords and scale runs—as for me, I prefer to keep chords, cadences, and scale runs in my head and not on paper. Usually, I look at my copy while I am taking my nightly bath, just before I hit the hay. There is a side effect. Studying the score just before I go to sleep sometimes troubles my sleep with the score haunting me as a visual image and the melody haunting me as an internal auditory phenomenon. When that happens too often, I skip studying the score before bedtime.

Advice: Studying the score just before bedtime often helps encode the material, though you may find your sleep disturbed by your brain working overtime when it should be resting. In that case, use your judgment about how much and when to study the score.

Writing Can Form Useful Associations and Can Work as a Memory Tool

When the score has some sections that present unusual difficulties, on a separate piece of paper I write out the chords measure for measure, sometimes assigning my own names to the chords as chunking tools.

For instance, in measure 59 of *Reverie* by Debussy, the start of the E major section, my notes say: Measure 59: three-finger chord start on A, three-finger chord on B, E Major first inversion, three-finger chord start on high E. Measure 60: three-finger chord start on A, three-finger chord start on B but with a triplet—chord F G—, E Major again first inversion, then down to E major in tonic form. Notice, I call the chords by the pattern position of my three fingers used to play them, as the pattern is the same for each although they start on different notes. Sometimes the pattern recognition is easier to recall than the name of the chords themselves. This is especially true in this piece by Debussy where lots of the chords are unconventional and have no routine name. Notice how narrative informs what needs to be played and the sequence.

Yes, it's okay to copy music for your personal use. Copying music, under the fair use rule, is legal if you have paid for the score and are using the copy for your own personal use. Even if you didn't pay, copying can be legal. All classical pieces have been out of copyright for over a hundred years. In fact, many pieces can be downloaded from the Internet for free for that reason: They are free; the copyright expired long, long ago, and anyone who tries to tell you differently is wrong. These great works are in the public domain for public use and will be in the public domain and public use until our sun burns out.

Seniors, Do Not Hide Behind Your Age

Some contests, festivals, and recitals allow adult students to play from notes whereas the younger students must play from memory. That is wrong. Every student should be on an equal footing and every student should be judged equally. No exceptions. The memory power of (some, not all) young people is pretty good. Even little children can repeat long poems and whole pages of books and (worse) the advertisements on radio and TV. But so can adults. This pall parrot memory is in all of us. Adults just tend to think they don't have it. And in a certain sense, they don't have it as much as they used to have it. Young people have highly impressionable minds and even small children like my granddaughter, Miranova (age two), can repeat by heart whole pages of a book of which she may have grasped the sense but dimly.

Because pall parrot memory tends to diminish with age, many people (including some well-known psychologists) convince themselves that after 35 (at the latest 40), it is useless to learn anything new. This belief in the decay of memory with age is highly convenient to the average mind, which is probably the author of it. Taking the line of least resistance, most people prefer to relax with the idea: "I am getting too old to memorize anything." Frankly, you are much better off carrying out the better idea: "Every day I am going to learn something new."

Those who pride themselves on their physique know that exercise is needed to maintain muscle tone, bulk, and power. Ditto for memory: Exercise is needed to maintain memory skills and memory power. Make sure you get it.

The (probably false) belief in the significant decay of memory with aging permits some adults to convince themselves that it is useless to try to memorize anything new. As mentioned, this attitude is self-defeating. If you think you can't do a thing, it is for sure that you will not be able to do it. Such thinking gets adult students to take the line of least resistance, most of them relaxing with the thought that "I am getting too old to learn." A better attitude is "Each new piece is a new adventure that must be learned anew. My mind, like my muscles, needs daily exercise and music is an ideal exercise for both mind and muscle. Boy, am I lucky."

Adult memory is a power that is useful and reliable. Let's give it a special dignity by giving it a special name: the selective memory of maturity.

If I can at age 82, joyfully undertake memorizing a sonata, so can others. Cato started learning Greek at age 80. Rumor has it that George W. Bush, after he left the office of President of the United States, actually read a book.

The power of a great memory depends upon habits of learning much more than is supposed; and in memory's growing obedience to the will is to be found the compensation for the passing years. Vladimir de Pachmann (Odessa 1848–Rome 1933) at age 70 said he was only beginning to learn how to practice and how to memorize music. Senior students, like maestro de Pachmann, need to find a sense of renewal, a sense of adventure, a sense of progress, and a sense of wonder by finding new methods, new pieces, new ways, new habits. Seniors need to hold fast to the spirit of youth, for that spirit will serve them best.

Bottom Line

Seniors, do not hide behind those grey hairs. Time spent in reconnoitering is never wasted.

Okay, let's get down to business. You have your piece in hand. What don't you do? What do you do?

Don't

By now you know what we are warring against: the mechanical customary process of memorizing by rote, i.e., playing the notes and repeating them until they are remembered. Without penetrating the design of the composer, it is very difficult and very time-consuming (and frequently impossible) to remember music that has not at first been mentally assimilated. Don't do it!

Do

By now you know what we are pushing for: an intellectual memory, as any form of complex memory must first start in the intellectual faculty. Therefore, learn as much about music theory as you can. Understanding scales, chords, cadences, measures, rhythms, and so forth is fundamental, for those things are the elemental materials of music. They give your mind the chunking techniques to more easily learn when you are trying to memorize. A student who can't differentiate between a broken chord and a passing note will find it difficult to pick out essentials. Much is missed without an intellectual appreciation of fugue and the beautiful devices that the tyros miss—imitation, inversion, stretto, and so forth. An appreciation of such things greatly simplifies learning by expanding your chunking tools and by expanding your meaningful associations.

Eventually, your music memory will greatly benefit from understanding all the major and minor scales with their common chords. Eventually, you must be able to play these and identify them readily. Fast identification and ability to play go hand in hand.

Study and Understand the Design of Your Piece

In music, the principal secret to aid mastery of a given passage consists in apprehending the design. When Liszt was asked how he memorized a new piece so quickly, he replied, "I apprehend the pattern." You must be able to apprehend the pattern, just like Liszt, and you must learn to hear it internally.

Actually do an analysis of your piece's parts, including chord progressions and phrases. Only then can you fully possess it mentally. Make sure you understand the overall musical design of your piece and the continuation or enlargement of this design according to the general principles that pertain to that design. The value of knowing the overall design is that you can't get lost while playing the piece because you will be mentally checking off the parts as they are done. The value of knowing the expected design is two-fold:

1. You will be able to anticipate what is going to happen and when—an important point because in music performance it pays to think ahead.

2. You will more easily remember when your piece deviates from the expected general design. The deviation or departure from the general plan would act as a nice memory peg and unique marker.

For instance: Does ABA mean anything to you? How about ABACA? What about minuet and trio? What key would you expect in the minuet part? What key in the trio? Why? And what part in minuet and trio is often repeated and when? What are the three main parts of a sonata?

The point is that the more you know, the more you can learn. Real pianists realize that music is an art form so complex and so deep that one can never know it all or master it all. Therefore, get ready for a lifetime of learning.

But What Do You Do If You Really Don't Know Something?

When you don't know something, look it up or ask your teacher. In other words, when you don't know, find out.

For instance, what if you run across a statement like this: "Baroque ornaments appear as ossias" and you are not sure what ossias are? Answer: You look ossias up in a dictionary.

The Oxford English Dictionary (OED) has no listing for ossias, so let's try ossia. Here, OED says that ossia is a conjunction that means "or else" and is usually used to indicate an alternative in a piece of music. The word comes from the Italian o sia, which means "or maybe." Following this up with a glance at the Collins Music Encyclopedia, we find ossia means "or" and is used to indicate an alternative (often easier) to a passage in a composition. The Harvard Dictionary of Music: Ossia (It). Or; used to indicate an alternative (often easier) version of a passage. Result: You now know something you didn't know before and that, friends, is progress.

Question: But what do you do when you don't understand a musical form?
Answer: Find out.

Ask your teacher. Look up the info someplace. The more you know about your piece, the composer, the period it was written, the expected structure, and so forth, the more personal associations you will be able to make and the easier it will be to recall and play the piece. You will also look smart, probably smarter than you are.

An Example from Chopin

Chopin's *Scherzo, Opus 24*. Nothing works better or is as valuable as the mental discipline of apprehending and executing musical designs, thus re-creating the composer's ideas and music. "Scherzo" is Italian for the word "joke." How does that help you approach the performance of this Chopin piece?

Chopin had tuberculosis and died of that disease. In some of his music, I sense aches and pains, fevers, night sweats, choking, coughing up blood, and terrible bone-numbing fatigue. But not in the *Scherzo*. Right? Why?

Listen to the Piece Played by Experts

There are many fine CD recordings of most major pieces. Listen to them over and over until you can tell exactly where the pianist is in the music and you can exactly predict what comes next. At first, listen while looking at the score and then listen without the score. Pay attention to themes, melodies, cadences, repetitions, and sequences. Assign labels to the various parts of the piece as you perceive them. The labels should relate to the sections of the piece and should help recall what should be played at that point.

This is truly a wonderful world where you can listen to wonderful pieces anywhere anytime. This privilege was not available to previous generations. You can listen informally while you are doing something else and you can listen attentively. You can listen to a CD with your teacher and discuss the performance as you both look at the score.

Jimmy White and I have listened to Sue Keller's interpretation of *Furry Lisa* and he gave me his input about the performance. We decided it was not a good piece for me.

The CDs play a role in my memory process and should play a role in your memory process. For instance, when memorizing *Blues in the Night* (music by Harold Arlen and words by Johnny Mercer), I sing along with the music. Some of the parts are music to match the words "my momma done tol' me" other parts match other words. I use the words as memory pegs. In *Blues in the Night* there is a section that sounds like train whistles. I call that section TRAIN. After the train comes a section in which Julie London sings about a nightingale. So, the label there is—guess?

After the nightingale section, there is an easy transition back to the beginning which repeats until measure 10, which goes directly to the section already labeled for you as the Coda (which we are informed means "little tail" in Italian). With the above in mind, how likely is it that I will get lost in playing *Blues in the Night*? Look at my YouTube version and see how confidently I play each section. What you don't see is the mental picture I have of the piece and the labeled structures that keep me oriented.

Repetition and Sequence

Repetition and sequence (sequence is a species of altered repetition) are keyed into the structure of music so prominently that whoever understands the principles and applications of them will unlock every piece. To master a piece quickly, you must reproduce a considerable portion of the music by means of sequence, repetition, or other methods of chunking the information. On a given page, the music will consist of a motive or a group of notes continued in sequence. As soon as the design is understood, you should be able to duplicate it on the keyboard, more or less without reference to the notes. This will be illustrated when we memorize *Fur Elise*. After repeating the design slowly, the actual notes should be learned without resorting to rote memory. After that, the task is to increase the speed gradually and add proper style and color to the performance.

Sequence

If the motive is a, b, c, d, the sequence could be b, c, d, e ascending and g, a, b, c having descended. An inverted sequence might be a, b, c, d, followed by the inversion d, c, b, a. If you recognize the pattern and know where to start, you automatically can play the notes without actually having memorized much. So, if I asked you to play this sequence four times ascending, it wouldn't be much trouble for you to do abcd, bcde, cdef, defg.

The Official Definition of Sequence

Looking up the word sequence in The Harvard Dictionary of Music, we find that Harvard thinks a sequence is the repetition of a phrase of melody (melodic sequence) or a harmonic progression (harmonic sequence) at different pitch levels, the succession of pitch levels rising or falling by the same or similar intervals. In a melodic sequence, the repetition occurs within a single voice. A melody may be transposed exactly, retaining its precise interval content and thus probably effecting a change of key, or the sequence may proceed diatonically, the melody retaining only its general contour and remaining in the same key. Thus spake Harvard. And that, folks, does cover the definition of sequence. You can tell a Harvard man, but you can't tell him much.

Whew! That's a lot of words for a definition, but not unexpected for something coming out of Harvard. My definition of sequence is shorter: "A musical idea repeated at different pitches." And Jimmy has a good one. To find out what, read on.

You Can Learn a Lot by Looking

Part of the job of memorizing the piece is understanding the features of the music you are studying. Do not begin by playing this motive that I have reproduced below. Begin by examining it carefully.

BERNARD M. PATTEN

Sonatina in C Major

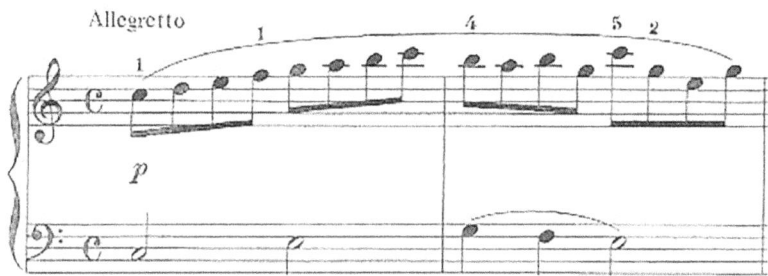

Every point and feature is to be observed, noted, and understood. Experienced pianists will get the information right away without giving it a second thought. New students should ask themselves questions to make sure the required observations are made and registered in the mind.

Practice making observations on measure one from *Sonatina in C Major* by Theodore Latour (1766–1837). Shout the answers out loud because that will have a greater chance of registering in your mind and being remembered. The idea is to focus your attention on the details of the music so that the information enters stage one of your memory. If you don't get this stuff in stage one, there is no hope that you will get it into stage two or stage three where you need it to remain. Furthermore, as playback requires stage one readout, every pianist must during performance have a point of attention and that point of attention had better be the piece and not any place else.

1. What clefs are shown?
2. What is the key? (Every key signature may represent a major or its relative minor. In the old days, composers frequently named their music by the form and the key as here. Therefore, we know that this is a Sonatina in C major. Ah, yes. But do we know what a Sonatina is? If not, what do we do to find out what a Sonatina is? Answer: Look it up or ask someone who knows—someone like your teacher.
3. What is the measure time signature? Can't find the time signature? Ask your teacher. It is there.
4. What tones of the key does the motive begin? This is very important. If you don't know where to start, you can't begin. Maria in *The Sound of Music* tells the Trapp children that "the beginning is a good place to start." She's right!

5. Describe the motive melodically. Is it a scale? A chord? Where is it going? Up? Down? Up and down? All around? How far?
6. Describe it rhythmically.
7. What dynamics are to be played? Hint: That little p means soft.
8. What is the value of the notes? Do they fill the entire measure or only part of it?
9. What phrasing is indicated to connect measure one and two? Should the measures be separate or played as one connected phase?

Wow! Isn't it amazing how much information is packed into the first two measures?

It is not my job to give you the answers to the above questions or to teach you how to read the info from the measures. It is the job of your teacher to teach you, and it is your job to know how to read the first two measures of a piece and how to get the information embedded there into your conscious mind. Work that stuff out with your teacher. And let me do my job, which is to prepare you to memorize the piece and to inform you that looking at the first two measures is the first step toward memory.

Just for Fun, Compare Your Answers to the Questions to Our Answers.

1. The treble and the bass clefs are shown.

2. The key is C major. That means expect most of the piece to involve tones of C major. Modulations to the V chord would involve G Major and to the IV chord to F Major. As the piece is called a Sonatina, expect that it is a small sonata. As a sonata, expect an exposition, a development, a recapitulation, and perhaps a coda. Expect the exposition to consist of two parts (binary form) with the first theme A followed by an almost identical A'. Next, expect a modulation to G or perhaps the relative minor A in part B. Part B should also be in binary form, let's say B followed by B'. Then, expect to return to part A in C major in binary form with A followed by a modified A, let's call it A''. The conclusion, as this is a piece from the classical era, should be an authentic cadence from G (V chord) to C (I chord or tonic). Thus, much of the large structure of this piece can be anticipated from the form name, Sonatina, and the indicated key. But why speculate? Look at the music. For your convenience, you can download a copy of the complete Sonatina free from www.musicstudents.com. This discussion is concerned only with

the Allegretto, but you can also look at the other two parts: the Pastorale and the Rondo, at your convenience.

Allegretto:

Theme A is in the key of C, and A' ditto. A and A' are four measures long and are identical except for the last measure of A and A', which differ. A and A' are then repeated exactly. B is also four measures long and is identical to B' except for the last measure of B and B'. B appears to be in the key of C except there is an F# in measure four of B. The key of C and G are identical except, of course, for this pitch. B and B' are not repeated. A follows, and a modified A (A''), which ends with the expected cadences from G to C.

So what?

So a lot.

Now I have a firm map of the large structure of this piece. But most of you out there in reader land do not. You did not download the piece because you were too lazy and therefore you missed some important points. Will you correct this deficiency or just let it ride? Laziness explains a lot of lack of progress in the real world. One of the keys to success in any field is work.

My mind will hang on to this map of the piece, and if memory serves correctly, I shall know where I am in the piece at all times. Furthermore, I see that A is repeated exactly three times and repeated almost exactly another three times, making 24 measures of A, taking more than half of the playing time. The difficulty will come trying to memorize the endings of A' and A''—those two measures, and the difficulty will come trying to memorize the ending measures of B and B'. The cadences at the very end make sense in terms of what we know should end the piece, so I don't anticipate much difficulty with them. Those cadences are in fact classical: Two third inversion G chords in the second half of measure 24 are followed by a first inversion C with the common note G expressed in the first half of measure 25. Are you lost? If so, it is because you did not do the work. Shame on you!

As expected, the common tone (G) is kept in the same voice, in this case, alto. As expected, the bass notes always reflect what is happening above: If the chord is G, the bass note is G; if the chord is C, the bass note is C.

Map Your Music

If you were asked to draw a crowded map from memory, you would not expect to recall it perfectly at first glance; you would have to go over the first impressions, possibly many times; each time with more and more attention to the details.

The same is true of your mental map of your music. Be patient when first learning a piece. No impression is lost. Your second view will take more readily, the third still more readily. If rightly spaced, your mind will learn with each repetition and review. But repetition, though needed, cannot take the place of conscious thought; and here you must not make the mistake that most students make. In order to memorize a map, looking at it frequently may not be enough. You must study it! You must think about it. You must associate what you know with what new information is depicted. To recall shapes exactly, you have to think about them, comparing one feature with another. If the courses of two rivers are somewhat alike, you must notice the differences and the conscious understanding of the differences will help you remember the map. So, this is the only way to easily remember music with certainty—to analyze it, making conscious associations and making a mental map of the music. Here are two passages that begin the same but end differently. Here is a phrase ending on the dominant, in contrast to another that ends on the tonic. This piece plays with the I-IV-V relationship and so forth.

You recall at will only what you notice, and nothing else. Train yourself to notice as much as you can, especially the similarities and differences, repetitions, and sequences, and the exact numbers of each in the piece and their location.

KNOWING STRUCTURE IS IMPORTANT

◆ ◆ ◆

Understanding the structure and identifying where the difficulties lie will give you a head start in studying those measures in detail. You will need to use some of the narrative and association techniques discussed previously for those challenging measures. You may have to learn them measure by measure, and if that proves difficult, you may need to learn them by intervals. Only in rare, desperate cases will you need to learn them chord by chord or note by note.

Try to understand the overall structure of your piece. For instance, if you are working on memorizing a fugue, you will be miles ahead if you keep in mind the general structure of the fugue, the subject, the counter subject, the episodes, and so forth. Structure is a magnificent way of chunking a large block of musical information without much effort and certainly with fewer tears.

Verification of the Analysis of the Sonatina in C Major

Looking at multiple YouTube recitals of this piece, I find that those who play it from memory get A and A' well but slow down or flub the last measure of B and B'. If you don't believe me, check it out yourself. At least now they can watch themselves and know exactly what they need to work on for next time.

Answers to the Questions Continued

1. The measure time signature is C, common time, also known as 4/4. There should be four beats to a measure, and each beat should be worth a quarter note. The eight eighth notes, therefore, make sense, and the division of the eighth notes into two groups of four reflects the human need to chunk. Note that the two half notes in the bass reflect the measure signature exactly, as each half note takes up half of the measure. A half is now and will forever be equivalent in time to two quarters as a mathematical fact. Isn't it wonderful in this uncertain world that some things are totally reliable, like $1/4 + 1/4 = 1/2$?

2. Attention! The answer to question four is the most important in your memory quest. You must recall where your piece starts, or you won't be able to play it, and you will be lost at the very beginning, unable to set in motion the automatic (non-declarative) memories that make up motor memory. In the case of this piece, the key of C gives a hint, as the starting tone in the bass and the starting tone in the treble are both C. But which C? That is easy to remember as each is one octave from middle C. One of my Mozart pieces starts on a high B. How do you plan to remember that fact? For me, it is sufficient to see in my mind's eye a picture of Mozart. On his head rests a bee; therefore, the B is high (for it's on his head). Of course, I shall recall the picture better if the bee is giving Mozart a sting and Mozart's face contorts in pain. Some students will, instead of constructing bizarre images to recall where things start, just memorize cold where the piece begins. They will be aided and

abetted in doing this by knowing the key, the general area of the piano involved, the expected pitch to be heard, and the visual image of their hands properly positioned over the starting keys.

Not only is it necessary for you to remember by one means or another where to start your piece, but it is also a good idea to memorize the starts of each of the separate parts of the piece as well. Memorize the notes by their letter name and memorize the start position by picturing in your mind's eye your hands on the piano in the exact position required to start each section. Do this for all the important parts of the piece: memorize the names of the note or notes or the chord that starts a section and memorize by visualization and tactile sensation where those starts are and how they feel and look. Eventually, when your playing of that piece has attained automaticity, you will forget the names of the notes and the names of the chords and just automatically put your hands in the right place and start playing.

If you have a lapse of memory, skip ahead (do not go back) to the next part that you know how to start. Skip to your lifesavers; let the lifesavers save your performance.

Repeat—Because This Is Important

Do yourself a favor and make sure you know how to start not only at the beginning of your piece but also at sections X, Y, and Z—the various places along in the piece. Know where these start positions are by encoding them in multiple modalities of memory: sound, tactile (hand position), and the visual appearance of your hands hovering over the correct keys. Consciously label or name the start position in some way to give a hook into the intellectual memory, just as I named the different sections of *Blues in the Night* so that it is impossible for me to confuse the TRAIN section with the NIGHTINGALE section.

Let's Pause for a Story About Memory Failure and Success

At a Veterans' Day ceremony, a nine-year-old student was supposed to recite the famous poem *In Flanders Fields* by Lieutenant Colonel John McCrae, MD. The Master of Ceremonies introduced the lad, who came to the podium, looked over the 6,000 eager faces in the audience, then paused for 20 seconds, made a face that expressed horror, and said in a panic, "I forgot my poem." It was a sad scene. This boy had probably recited that poem hundreds of times at home. What he may have needed was the first line of the poem, which he could have easily read from the program as the title of the poem begins the first line. After that first line, automatic memory might have carried him through. But we will never know. They didn't give him a second chance. They pulled him off.

Another boy, about the same age (nine or ten), who had just finished reciting Lincoln's *Gettysburg Address,* stepped forward, volunteered to fill in, and flawlessly recited McCrae's poem.

Wow! What a demonstration. It turned out that the other boy, the one who did both recitations, had, over a seven-month period, practiced both Lincoln's address and *In Flanders Fields* literally thousands of times. That boy's great-uncle (who at the time was a senator) trained the boy to recite both the address and the poem. The senator had reasoned that the kid doing *Flanders* might clutch, in which case the senator's nephew could step right in. And that is exactly what happened.

Question: why in the world am i telling you this story?

Question: what in the world does recital of an address or a poem have to do with playing music or memorizing music?

Stop for two minutes. Put your feet up on the desk, or go get a Coke or cup of tea, or pace the floor. Think up answers to the questions. Then compare your answers to mine.

Answers: Dr. Patten told us the story because he likes stories and thinks stories teach great lessons, especially when the stories are true. The lessons apply to music recitals because, in many ways, poetry recitation and music recital are similar. The features they share are:

1. They both involve musical instruments. In one case, the human voice is a string instrument that is activated by human breath. In the other case, the musical instrument is the piano, which is a string instrument activated by hammers hitting the strings.

2. Both recitation and recital are in public places in front of an audience and both require memory and not only direct intelligent expression of meaning but also expression of emotion.

3. We learn what is correct by knowing what is not correct. In the case of the boy who failed, we learn that better preparation might have helped. And it is an acknowledged fact that better preparation would save lots of music recitals as well. We think the boy who failed might have been

cued or clued by the first lines of the poem. Knowing the first notes of your music will set you on the right track. It is an acknowledged fact that if you don't know where to start, you will have trouble starting. And if you can't start, you sure as hell can't finish. We also understand that the brain of the boy who failed was in a different chemical state from the state in which his brain had encoded the poem. Review the sections on state-dependent learning if you feel vague on how this applies to music recitals. Thus, the boy who failed probably failed for many reasons, among which were stage fright, altered brain state, and inadequate preparation.

4. We learn what is correct by copying the success of what is correct and the methods used to get to that success. In the case of the boy who flawlessly recited the address and the poem, we learned that there was an enormous amount of preparation involved, much more than anyone would have imagined. According to the senator uncle, the practice sessions were always done in front of a mirror so that the boy himself could see his performance. The uncle would correct body posture, hand gestures, facial expressions, tone, tempo, pace, diction, and so forth. In other words, the preparation for recitation was on a high, almost professional level. We also saw how an experienced public speaker like the senator could predict, and in fact did predict, with remarkable accuracy, the likely failure of a young and very inexperienced speaker who would be set before an assembled multitude the likes of which that boy had never seen before or imagined.

Senatorial Overkill?

Furthermore, to train the nephew to control stage fright, the senator arranged for the nephew to do the recitation before several different audiences, including the Chamber of Commerce and the Elk's Club. The senator asked the school principal at the nephew's elementary school to arrange for the recitation to take place before a general assembly of students and teachers. That happened also. In addition, on the day before Veterans' Day, the senator and the nephew visited the venue where the recitation was to take place. The venue was a large public park, and the men had already put up a platform that would overlook the assembled crowd. The nephew did a recital from that platform. And, (get this, this really impressed me) the senator inquired as to where the ceremony might take place in the event of rain. The senator and the nephew then went to the Queens Theatre, the rain venue, two blocks away and recited the two items from the stage of the dark and empty theater.

On Veterans' Day, the rain started just as the Lincoln's Gettysburg Address was to go on. The announcement was made and a half-hour later, the program started again, this time inside the theater where the nephew had rehearsed the day before. Was this overkill? In a certain sense, it was. But in another sense, it wasn't. The senator was training the nephew to become an accomplished public speaker. The recitation preparation was a preparation, not just for this event on Veterans' Day, but also for a lifetime of political activity that the senator had envisioned for his nephew. The senator knew the value of over-preparation and the value of practicing as close as possible to performance conditions.

Remember: Practice should simulate playback conditions as closely as possible. If a phrase is meant to be soft, why practice it loudly? To play softly is not easy because it requires strict control of motor habits. Why should a melody be practiced as a succession of even notes if the composer intended it to sing with varied tones above a soft accompaniment? If a passage has four notes to the beat, why rehearse in triplets? Apart from these considerations, expression is a great help to the memory. Actors with the best memory for words are those who concentrate on their meaning, associating expression through voice and gesture. You should try to do the same in practice: Associate musical expression with every note played.

Back to the Latour Sonatina

The initial measure is of course the C Major octave. Instead of memorizing the individual notes that you must play in succession (cdefgabc), you chunk it by starting on C and play the C major scale. While you are playing the C Major scale, you can place a C in the bass with the initial treble C in measure one and a bass E note with the fifth note of the scale (G). While you are automatically playing the C Major scale, you can get yourself ready for the easy descending sequences to follow that start in measure two. The p in measure one of course indicates the initial part is to be played softly. The other questions should be easy to answer so let's not bother with them and let's go on to review some memory items that apply to music memory.

Review the Neurophysiology of Learning

At this point, it might be helpful to review some of the facts of human memory as explained in part one. As you do this, think of how those facts could be applied to your music memory tasks. In a little while, we will go over some of the items that we think are important. What you do yourself will be much more helpful to you than anything that I can do for you. So why not actually go over the items in part one and apply them to your situation? If you don't do it now, when will you?

Before Getting to Some Tips, Let's Answer Two Important Questions That Come Up Occasionally:

1. How long will it take for me to memorize my piece?
2. How long will the piece remain in my memory once I have memorized it?

Most students don't ask these questions, but some do. When they do, they usually get an answer that sounds like this: "As long as necessary" or "Much longer than you think."

Such answers, while true, tend to beg the question and certainly are not scientific as they do not lend themselves to experimental verification. Science requires actual verification. Qualitative and vague answers need to be replaced by something quantitative and definite. What is needed to answer the questions is some actual data from some actual experiments designed to find out how long it takes to memorize a piece of music and how long (once it is memorized) that piece will remain in the memory.

Dr. Patten's Preliminary Results of Experimental Studies of Music Memory

Dr. Patten: In order to study music memory quantitatively, I followed the protocol of Hermann Ebbinghaus, except I didn't memorize meaningless words and I didn't lock myself in my room. I memorized (what else?) music and sat (where else?) at the piano. I recorded the time spent in the process. When I was able to play the piece twice without an error, I considered the piece in my memory. Then, just as Ebbinghaus did, I tested myself at periodic intervals to see how much of the piece remained in the memory over time. My aim was to get forgetting curves for music so that those curves for music memory could be compared and contrasted with the classical forgetting curves for unassociated verbal material as first discovered by Ebbinghaus. Unlike Ebbinghaus, I had the physical means of recording my performances and followed the playback with the score. If there was a single wrong note in a measure, that measure was counted as an error. The percent measures correct was the percent of correct measures in the whole piece that were played note perfect. Thus, even if there was only one false note in a measure, I counted the whole measure as an error. Thus, the percent retention is a worst-case estimate of retained music because usually there was only one wrong note in the measures that were graded wrong. In most cases, such wrong notes would not be detected by the usual audience under the usual performance circumstances.

The data on some of the pieces that I memorized is presented below. Right now before giving you the data, I want to talk about the results. In the results, there is good news and there is bad news. First, the good news:

The Good News About Music Memory

Music memory is solid and decays only slightly with time. It certainly does not decay anywhere near as much or as quickly as verbal memory as shown in the forgetting curve first published by Ebbinghaus. Why this is the case is not known. But the data is unequivocal on this fact. This means once you have learned to play your piece from memory, it is highly likely that that piece will remain in your memory more or less intact for at least a week. The magnetic resonance images of the brain done on practice memory do show the same considerable savings of memory tracts. Only at about two weeks do we see significant loss of memory if there is no rehearsal. Rehearsal renews the memory by freshening and reconfirming the synapses in the brain. Therefore, if you wish to keep your repertoire in your memory, it is a good idea to actually play your repertoire once a week. Experts might get away with a review once every two weeks, but for real security, once a week is needed.

My practice has been to play my entire repertoire every Sunday. If there is trouble or hesitations or mistakes, I consult the notes after I have gone through the piece as best I could. If a piece is not played correctly, I work on it until it is played correctly. The amount of time involved is minimal compared to the amount of time that was needed to get the piece in the memory in the first place. Once learned, pieces can be polished quickly even if not played for years. Scientific studies clearly show that the relearned piece will have a different and much-prolonged forgetting curve, which brings us to some bad news.

The Bad News About Music Memory

To get music in the memory requires a great deal of skill, hard work, and time. The experience with memory tasks has been that the longer the piece, the more complicated the piece, the fewer the repeats, and the greater the note density (that is, the average number of notes per measure), the more unique measures, and the faster the piece is to be played, are all items that increase the time and work needed to get the piece firmly into the memory. These, therefore, are the enemies of memory: long pieces, complicated pieces, few repeats, high note density (Jimmy says lots of black on the sheet), unique measures, unusual chords, and fast tempo. Overcome these difficulties by slow practice to educate the fingers and multiple exercises on the difficult parts until mastered. Instead of doing Hamon exercises, you are exercising on real pieces and thus making progress on real music.

Estimations Are Approximations

Those of you who took a course in logic will recognize the above statement as a tautology. It is like saying bachelors are unmarried or imports come from other countries. The undecided can go one way or the another. How long it will take to memorize a piece depends on so many variables that the best you can come up with is an estimation, and that estimation will be an approximation.

Conclusion: You Will Not Be Able to Predict Exactly How Long It Will Take to Memorize a Given Piece

Two rules of thumb that work for me might also work for you. Rule one is a guesstimation based on the Fermi equations for guessing. (Yes, these come from the same atomic scientist whose name you know so well. His hobby was predicting events by sophisticated guessing, and the technique is called Fermi guesstimation.)

Fermi Guesstimation

Look at your piece and estimate the minimal amount of time you think you will need to get the piece firmly in your memory. After you have quantitative data on your own experience with many pieces, your estimate of this minimal time will be more accurate. Then estimate the maximal time that you think it will take to learn the piece. Multiply minimal time by maximal time and then take the square root of the answer. This is the geometric mean, which Fermi has discovered is a more accurate predictor than the arithmetic mean.

Thus, Madge, my teacher, told me to memorize a piece called *Carnival Rag* by Mona Rejino. Looking over the piece and doing an analysis of the repeats and organization, I estimate it will take a minimum of three hours and a maximum of five hours to memorize. Thus, the Fermi guesstimation would be 3 x 5 = 15 and the square root of 15 is 3.87 hours or three hours and 52 minutes. On *Morning Song* by Cornelius Gurlitt (1820-1901) (see data below), the minimum was three hours and the max was also five. But, stupid me, did not see the ABABA structure initially, so the estimate had to be revised to one hour minimum and three maximum for an estimate of the square root of three or 1.73 hours or one hour and 44 minutes. This estimate came in under the actual time, which was one hour and 22 minutes.

Patten Guesstimation

Experience is a great teacher. My experience is that the time to complete memorization is not linearly related to the length of the piece or to the number of measures, but it is strongly correlated with the number of unique measures and less strongly correlated with the average number of notes per measure, which I call note density. Empirically, multiplying the number of unique measures by two and then multiplying the result by the note density will give an estimation of the number of minutes needed to memorize the piece. Thus, *Morning Song* has only 11 unique measures and a note density of eight, giving a Patten guesstimation of 2 x 11 = 22 x 8 = 176 minutes as the time needed to get the piece into the memory. The actual time that it took to memorize this piece was 82 minutes. Applying the same formula to *Scarborough Fair*, we get 44 x 5 = 220 minutes, which matches the 217 minutes I actually needed. *Blues in the Night* had 34 unique measures and a note density of ten, so the estimation was 680 minutes. The actual time to memorize this classic blues piece was 745 minutes.

How to Calculate the Number of Unique Measures and the Note Density

Copy the piece. Start at the beginning and look at each measure. When you come to a measure that is exactly the same as a measure that you have already seen, put an X through the duplicate measure. Do this for the entire piece and then count the number of measures that have no X. For the note density, just eyeball the first page and estimate the average number of notes per measure.

Here's some data from memory studies by me. Recall that the criterion was perfect performance twice. Time to less than perfect performance would be less, in some cases much less:

Morning Song By Cornelius Gurlitt (1820-1901)

Total Time to Criterion: 82 Minutes
Key: F Major
Study Time Breakdown: five sessions on five separate days over a seven-day period, average session 16.4 minutes, range seven to 22 minutes
Measures: 40
Notes: 307
Unique Measures: 11
Average Notes per Measure: eight by eyeball (calculated value actually counting each measure and averaging was pretty close at 7.675 notes per measure)
Comment: ABABA form makes for easy organization. The first two measures of A exactly repeat as measures four and five of A. The first two measures of B exactly repeat as measures four and five of B.

Memory Retention (time values are after the piece has been played perfectly twice):
At criterion: 100% correct twice
One hour—90% (36 measures correct out of 40)
24 hours—90%
48 hours—90%
72 hours—not tested
96 hours—95%
120 hours—not tested
144 hours—not tested
168 hours—90%

Conclusion: The forgetting curve for music memory is quite different (and much better) than the forgetting curve for unassociated three-letter meaningless combinations.

Scarborough Fair by Anonymous circa 1625

Total Time to Criterion: 217 Minutes
Key: Listed as d minor, but actually probably dorian mode as Bb's are all natural.
Study Time Breakdown: 14 sessions on 14 separate days over a 22-day period, average session 15.5 minutes, range three to 20 minutes.
Measures: 42
Notes: 229
Unique Measures: 22
Average Notes per Measure: five by eyeball (actual calculated value 5.452)
Comment: Middle part repeats exactly, but the treble is an octave higher in the second repeat.

Memory Retention:
At criterion: 100% correct twice
24 hours—93% (39 measures correct out of 42)
48 hours—not tested
72 hours—not tested
96 hours—93%
120 hours—93%
144 hours—100% (note perfect!)
168 hours—95%
Nine days post criterion—100% after a 22-minute review at the piano.

Conclusion: Review time is well spent. Music memory is pretty good.

Blues in the Night by Harold Arlen (words by Johnny Mercer): Total Time to Criterion: 745 Minutes

Key: C Major
Study Time Breakdown: 40 sessions over a 53-day period, average session 18.6 minutes, range four to 50 minutes. Usually, there was only one session per day but on 9/8/2008 there were two sessions: 10-10: 10 AM & 10: 10-10: 30 PM; there were two sessions on 9/14: 2: 00-2: 30 & 4: 00-4: 50; two sessions on 9/20 2: 06-2: 36 & 9: 30-9: 40; there was

one mental review on 9/22 lasting eight minutes, and there were three sessions on 9/23 4: 07-4: 20, 7: 57-8: 01 & 8: 10-8: 18
Measures: 53
Notes: 525
Unique Measures: 34
Average Notes per Measure: 10 by eyeball (calculated value 9.906)
Comment: Memorization started on September 5, 2008 and actually reached only two wrong notes on September 23. So the piece was pretty much in the memory after 494 minutes of work. The bulk of the rest of memory training time was thus spent trying to reach the criterion of 100% note perfection.

Memory Retention
At criterion: 100% correct twice
24 hours—96%
48 hours—not tested
72 hours—98% (left out D on page 3)
96 hours—not tested
120 hours—not tested
144 hours—92%
168 hours—90%
192 hours—100% after a 13-minute review at the piano

Minuet in G Major from the Notebook of Anna Magdalena Bach (1725)

Study time breakdown and other data were stolen with Dr. Patten's Lincoln when it was parked in Jackson, Mississippi on 11/30/2008, but a copy of the memory retention data was left at home.

Memory Retention
At criterion: 100% correct twice
One hour—98%
24 hours—not tested
46 hours—98%
72 hours—not tested
96 hours—not tested
120 hours—not tested
144 hours—not tested
168 hours—80%
192 hours (that is, eight days post criteria) 80%
192 hours after a ten-minute review of the piece: 100% (note perfect)

Comment: Perhaps the absence of the testing on days three, four, five, and six led to a degradation in the memory. On day eight (192 hours), the performance that immediately followed a ten-minute review at the piano was 100% note perfect.

Summary of Advice and Some Tips About Your Music Memory

What follows are some suggestions for you to consider. If they make sense to you, you might apply them in your next memory task. If they don't seem to make sense, then go on to the next idea and evaluate its utility. You are the ultimate judge of what is good and what is not so good for your memory training. Part three of this book will have a specific example of how to memorize a piece by Beethoven. For the nonce, we wish to just display some ideas for your critical appraisal.

1. Memorize at regular intervals, just as you would practice at regular intervals. An hour a day is a good idea. But a better idea is four 15-minute periods distributed throughout the day.

2. Work on pieces that you understand and like and that are within your technical ability. All people, young or not, play best and memorize best that music that they like. Start to memorize only after you and your teacher agree you are playing well enough from notes. If you don't have a teacher, get one. Significant progress without a teacher is unlikely.

3. Study the music in detail, outlining the different parts. Pay attention to the imitations, repetitions, sequences, chords, and so forth. Mentally label the main parts of the piece with names that will help you recall by association where you are and what you are playing. Each section should be embedded in your memory independently so that you can start at that section if you need to. Usually, you might have to divide a major classical piece into five or six parts. When you feel that you have the entire piece in the memory, roll a die and play whatever part comes up on the die face. That way you know that you can move ahead to any part if you become lost or break down.

4. If there is any department of piano playing where you should follow your own judgment, it is that of fingering. The best teachers will tell you that. Choose a fingering that suits both your hand and the passage played. Try every fingering that occurs to you and choose what works best for you. Aim for a relaxed harmony among fingers, arm, and body posture. There is an old saying: "One is never better served than by oneself."

Once chosen, the fingering should not be altered as that may throw your motor memory off. At this point, you should realize that motor (muscular) memory is treacherous. Unless you use the same fingering each and every time you play the piece, confusion may arise as to which muscles are to do the work. As a result, breakdown may occur. If you are committing a piece of music to memory, and it is not fingered in your copy, finger any doubtful passages yourself and keep rigidly to your own fingering. If your hand is smaller or larger than average, the suggested fingering may not be optimal for you. In that case, make the appropriate changes and stick with them. The greater the distance of the notes from middle C, the more likely muscular memory will fail. There is a neurophysiologic reason for this phenomenon that is embedded in the structure of the brain's motor cortex. Therefore, in practicing the piece, the student must memorize these far notes intellectually—that is to say consciously, in order to know exactly where to go. As a general rule, whenever arm muscles are brought into play, memorize consciously. The arm muscles lack the nervous system control mechanisms needed for precision, accuracy, and delicacy of movement and motor memory and motor control that is the common possession of hand, fingers, and wrist. Much practice and detailed training may change this for you, but until it does, you would be well served to follow the advice above.

5. When memorizing, concentrate on one thing at a time. It is not possible for the average student to learn a whole sonata at once. Do what the Romans did: Divide and conquer. Memorize by sections and the logical divisions that you discovered in your study of the organization of the piece. Try to memorize by phrases or longer musical divisions and not bar by bar. Stay flexible. Sometimes you will be able to memorize an eight-measure phrase at once, but other times you will be dealing with only two measures. And sometimes you may have to focus your entire attention on one measure or even a half measure until you get it memorized. Use the tricks when you are stuck: tell a story, narrate to yourself the note sequences and changes, make associations, make up words to the melody and sing along, and so forth. Unnecessary far-fetched mnemonics are not needed. The association of song with music can certainly help you understand phrasing, but to associate ridiculous words and images with noble music is probably counterproductive. You are a unique, individual person. There is no one on this planet before or after you that is or will be exactly like you. As an individual, you must learn to think about your music in an individual way that suits you and you alone. Whatever the teacher suggests as a link or association to promote memory should be left to you to add or detract and to form according to your own temperament. Advanced students will find that linking with color (research papers have been written on this idea known as chromaesthesia) helps; others appreciate music in abstract patterns

(that's me). As your music memory progresses, you will find that it is not necessary to use a story or pictures to get items in the memory. Most music books for children are probably illustrated with that idea in mind.

As for me, I like a plain grown-up appearance to the sheet music as I find the verses and illustrations distracting. I also don't like the teacher to scribble reminders on my sheet music. In my view, that is a distraction and not an aid to memory so much as it is a hindrance. Some teachers will take exception to my view and scribble everything they can think of on the sheets. To each his own preference, and I know mine. What's yours?

6. Once all the sections are in the memory, it is easy to put the whole thing together.

7. Memorize phrasing and dynamics as carefully as you memorize the notes.

8. Review frequently and test yourself by playing the passage in question to prove that you know it. Remember: There is a major difference between what we think we know and what we actually do know. When unsure, consult the notes to verify that you played it right or to verify that you played it wrong. Correct mistakes immediately so that you do not memorize the mistakes. The hazard of repetition is that repeating what is wrong actually gets memorized because the brain doesn't know anything and doesn't care. It is just a coincidence machine. Remember: Practice tends to make permanent, but only perfect practice tends to make permanent perfect. Also, remember that perfect is the enemy of the good. In most real-world cases, you don't need to be perfect because good will be good enough. And the enormous work to get to perfect is often not worth the marginal improvement in the overall effect on your audience. The sooner you realize that most things in life are compromises, the better off you will be. Sometimes less is more, and more is just too much.

9. Make videos of your performances so you can document your progress or lack of progress and you can view and understand your mistakes. Using the information from the video, polish your stage presence and performance. If you don't know what's good, how can you preserve it? If you don't know what's bad, how can you correct it? There is nothing bad that can't be corrected: Hamlet, reasoning with his mother Gertrude on the topic of dropping a bad habit and substituting a good one, said: "For use almost can change the stamp of nature." Here Hamlet was misquoting Aristotle, who said, "Use can change the stamp of nature."

10. Follow the advice of the master teacher Tobias Matthay and "Always think of the music from the bass up."

Well, I don't know about always. Always covers lots of territory, perhaps too much. But you get the general idea. In general, memorizing the bass first and then attaching the treble helps facilitate memory. Usually, the bass has a more consistent pattern and therefore can be more easily chunked into the memory. Then when the bass pattern is in the memory, the newer material (melody, for instance, or harmony) can be attached to it, taking advantage of the memory trick of using the bass as a memory peg. If the pattern is simpler in the treble, then reverse the method and memorize the easier pattern first and attach the harder to it. When we come to memorizing *Fur Elise,* you may see how helpful this approach can be.

11. Don't let one failure or several failures stop you. There are plenty more failures where they came from. If a passage continues to defeat you, leave it until tomorrow. Don't be upset if you seem to have forgotten what you played well yesterday. That is normal. Don't be surprised if what you thought you would never master suddenly seems to play itself. That's what happened to me today with Chopin's *Valse 64 no. 2.* Last night I couldn't play it right to save my life. Today it was perfect! That's normal too. The unconscious mind is always working and may come up with solutions that you didn't think possible. This is the tip-of-the-tongue phenomenon applied to music memory. Did that tip-of-the-tongue ever happen to you? You wanted to recall a name or a fact and you knew it was close at hand but just couldn't bring it to consciousness. And then, sometime later, the item pops into consciousness.

12. Aim for accuracy. Speed and facility will follow. Use the metronome to steady your pulses and rhythm if you must, but beware playing like a robot. Good control of beat is important in dance pieces, and as most baroque music descends from dance, you may want to use the metronome more when working on the baroque masterpieces. Or you may not want to use the metronome. The choice is yours.

The metronome should not inhibit your expressiveness because you (if you are like me) won't use it much. Josef Hofmann did not approve of the use of the metronome. He wrote: "You should not play with the metronome for any length of time, for it lames the musical pulse and kills the vital expression in your playing. Tempo is so intimately related to touch and dynamics that it is in a large measure an individual matter. Consult your own feeling for what is musically right in deciding upon the speed of a piece."

13. When you are close to complete memory of the piece, try playing the most difficult parts first. Concentrate more on the middle of the piece, as the middle is usually the hardest to master and the place that will cause the most trouble during performance. Most times when I do this, I realize I neglected the middle section—didn't label it or forgot to memorize its organization, and so forth.

Remember the serial position effect? The human brain tends to recall best the things that are presented first and last and tends to forget the middle things most. To compensate for this fact, we must spend more time and give more attention to the middle sections of the piece. Middle sections also are sometimes the more complex and thus do in and of themselves require more time and work to get them into the memory.

14. Work on improving one part of the piece at a time. Once you are note perfect, work on tone color, legato, and pedaling as isolated tasks, and then put things together. Remember that due to the limitations of stage one memory, it is often not possible to concentrate focused attention on more than one thing at a time. Perfect the individual items by focused attention, and then, later, integrate the items into the whole performance.

15. End each session by playing the piece correctly from notes. Recall the serial position effect: The first items and the last items in a series are remembered best, so make sure you got the middle section correct.

16. Relax while at the same time pretending that you are actually doing the piece before a vast and highly critical audience. That imaginary play-acting may condition you to deal with performance anxieties. Relaxed muscles may help relax the mind. Get rid of that tense facial structure, posture, and tone quality. Complete relaxation during performance is not possible, of course, but getting yourself in the right mental state of "attention minus effort" will bring body and mind into a condition free from strain and will help you perform the right way.

17. Concentrate your full attention on the piece and nothing but the piece. Do not try to think too far ahead in the piece lest you distract yourself from the present performance task. Let the music steer the playing to what comes next.

And for heaven's sake, avoid the thought that routinely fouls me up: "Oh, look at me! I am playing so well. This is just great." When sight-reading, you have to look ahead and think of the music ahead of your fingers. To consciously do this when playing from memory is the greatest mistake of all. In the experience of every public performance that I have given, most of the breakdowns have been caused by congratulating myself on how well I am playing or worrying about what note or passage is next. Interfered with by doubt, motor habits break down, and I blame memory when all that I needed was faith in myself.

Sidebar on Why Attention Is Important

The Maharajah of Jaipur, about to choose a Prime Minister, announced that he would only appoint the man who walked around the walls of the city holding a bowl filled to the brim with milk without spilling a drop. A number of men, yelled at, laughed at, jeered, frightened, or otherwise distracted, tried and failed the task. "Those are no Prime Ministers," said the Maharajah of Jaipur.

Then came another, whom no scream, no threat, no distraction could take his attention from the task or his eyes from the rim of the bowl.

"Fire!" said the captain of the troops.
They fired, but nothing was spilled.
"There is my real Prime Minister," said the Maharajah.
"Did you hear the cries?" asked the Maharajah.
"No."
"Did you see the attempts to frighten you?" asked the Maharajah.
"No."
"Did you hear the shots?" asked the Maharajah.
"No. I was watching the milk."
Point of story: When you are fully concentrating, nothing will distract you.

18. Get it out of your head that you are going to forget. That is a dangerous idea. If you think you are going to forget, the chances are very good that you will forget. If you have a thought about forgetting, switch your attention to the rhythm and to expression. Repeat: Forget about forgetting. Concentrate your full attention on the performance.

19. If you do forget when practicing, play through to the end and then immediately go to the notes and correct the problem. Try to figure out the cause of the mistake. Make a narrative or better still understand the pattern that will help prevent the same mistake from happening again. Study the defective passage in detail. Organize your study by individual modalities: Visualize the correct notes, hear the correct notes in your mind, place your hands and fingers on the correct keys and go through the correct series while fixing the image of your hands in the correct positions, and last but not least use your conscious intellectual analysis

of the problem area so that you can invoke intellect and conscious understanding when all else fails. Follow the rules of memory and you will do well. Don't follow the rules and you risk failure. The laws of human memory are binding on all without exception. Woe to those who break them.

20. When performing in recital or contests, should you forget—fake it! Improvise!If you can't improvise, do not go back. For heaven's sake, do not start again at the beginning. Go on to your predetermined lifesaver and don't forget to smile and act like everything is copacetic.

21. Avoid thinking of notes. Think of sounds, melody, phrases, intervals, but name notes only as a last resort. Naming notes is like naming the letters in Lincoln's *Gettysburg Address*—a waste of time and a thing that is likely to stall the performance.

22. Rest between repetitions. Walk around. Go to a different room. Wring your hands. Even if you do this for only 15 seconds, your brain will be more likely to approach the next repetition with relish rather than boredom.

23. Don't worry about repeating the same piece over and over. But do try to get something out of it each time you do repeat. Moriz Rosenthal, one of the great technicians of all time, told Charles Cooke that after studying Chopin's brief simple masterpiece, *Prelude in A, No. 7, Opus 28* for 60 years, he still found deeper levels of beauty in it.

Repair of Fractures—Orthopedics as Applied to Music Memory

Orthopedics is the medical specialty that aims to straighten children and keep them straight. That's what the word means. Ortho = straight; peds refers to children. And that is how this great specialty in ancient times got started. Now orthopedics is a surgical science concerned with not only straightening children and keeping them straight, but the general repair and maintenance of bones and joints. A practice division of orthopedics concerns the setting of fractures.

So what?

At some point in the memorization of your piece, you will play and record your performance and review that performance. Here's the advice: Play the piece straight through from memory, forcing yourself as best you may through any passages of unusual difficulty. This will give you a valuable total impression of the piece and an idea of where the "fractures" are. Every place where you stop or falter is, in greater or less degree, a fracture, compound or simple fracture, that needs to be set properly. Surgeons know that the properly set fracture will heal and become stronger than the adjacent bony regions. So setting is the correct treatment.

Mark off on your copy of the score that you made for yourself each and every fracture and mark the measures before and after the fracture site. Knowing what comes before and after the fracture is essential to your associative memory. If you have too many fracture sites marked off, especially if most of the piece is a collection of fractures, give up. That piece is too difficult for you to play at this stage of your progress. Now tell yourself that you are going to repair the fracture so that it will become the strongest part of your performance.

Using the notes, play the fractures one at a time, many times, paying attention to everything: the measures before and after, the correct notes (especially sharps and flats), time values, dynamics, touch (legato, staccato), and so forth until the fracture site is set and played better than the other parts of the piece. This is never going to be dull work. It is going to be fun and lively and absorbing, requiring your full concentration and attention. It will give you joy, the joy of memorizing a piece in its entirety, a joy that can well be described as holy.

Although the language in the last paragraph seems overblown, I can tell you that as a physician there is a great joy in setting a fracture or suturing a wound, a joy that could well be described as holy. In my view, one of the key features in perfecting any great skill is the recognition and correction of mistakes. That's what fracture setting is all about: The recognition and correction of a mistake. Igor had a personal view of this situation that coincides with mine:

"I have learned throughout my life as a composer chiefly through my mistakes and pursuits of false assumptions, not by my exposure to founts of wisdom and knowledge." *Igor Stravinsky (1882-1971)*

BERNARD M. PATTEN

FRACTURE SETTING
❖ ❖ ❖

The general rule for fracture setting: If the work of one hand is easy, begin by learning the easy hand. We will see the application of this rule in *Fur Elise*. Memorize that hand quickly, as you would memorize the A drone in *Fur Elise*. Then you can (almost) forget it while you work on the hard hand part of the fracture. This keeps it simple and prevents stage one overload. That way, more of your stage one memory will be available to focus on the difficult sections. In most fractures, the left hand's work is simple, with most of the difficulties falling on the right hand, as we will see when we memorize what's coming up.

Advanced Musicology

Before we get to the next volume of this book, where we apply our memory techniques to actual pieces, we will explore a few advanced concepts in musicology along with some tidbits and doodads. I saved this section for later because I knew these concepts might be off-putting if introduced too early. However, if you've made it this far in the book, you might benefit from a more advanced view of music before diving into actual memorization. This section will cover assorted topics including cadenzas, chromatic scales, and more. I hope you find it helpful, and if it seems difficult, take it slow and absorb a little at a time. Your teacher may be able to assist you, or perhaps you'll solve the challenges on your own. Practice productive thinking and learn to generate answers for yourself as early in your music career as possible. Solving practical problems is creative work, and it can also be fun.

Ready? Set? Let's go!

What Are Cadenzas For?

Believe it or not, cadenzas at the end of classical pieces or sections of pieces were intended as invitations for the performer to create their own endings in the style of the composer and the piece. The idea was not to go to some music library and hope to learn a cadenza written by some composer or pianist of the past. In the baroque era (c. 1600-1750), the accomplished pianist would typically perform the piece as written and then repeat it with added embellishments to showcase their skill and entertain the audience. In fact, many of Bach's pieces started as improvised works and were written down later. Several musical styles actually call for improvised sections, such as music from Spain, Mexico, Africa, and India, as well as Jewish, gypsy, jazz, blues, black gospel, southern gospel, and swing music.

Yes, improvisation is nice to know and even nicer to do. But just as with so-called extemporaneous public speeches, you need to have some training and know what is likely to work and what won't. It also helps to have some boilerplate dialogue and perhaps a few jokes ready for your "extemporaneous" speech. It's easy to adapt what you've already prepared and carry things off in almost any situation, making it seem as if you are thinking on your feet. Since I have many public speaking opportunities, I keep six Irish stories, five good jokes, a three-minute roast, and a five-minute funeral oration in my head. Lately, the funeral orations have been in demand as many of my friends keep insisting on dying. At the end of my funeral oration, I recite the famous poem *No Man is an Island.* You can listen to it on my YouTube channel, Bernard Patten.

Public Speaking and Music Performance—An Analogy

Under Jimmy's instructions, I've been trying to approach my music in the same way I approach public speaking—by being my natural self. I have a good grasp of how to play *Blues in the Night*, for instance, and can ad-lib on some of the major passages depending on how I feel and how I gauge the audience's mood. Some audiences enjoy a lot of variation in tempo, while others prefer emphasis on the black notes that aren't usually part of the C major key in which the piece is written. However, these notes are definitely part of the blues scale, and somehow the audience recognizes it. Some audiences prefer a straightforward rendition. My wife, Ethel, loves the nightingale part with emphasis, so I repeat that part several times for her. Jimmy likes me to play the blues scale at the end of the piece, starting way up high, descending, and finally ending on C major in treble and bass. I enjoy that ending as well and now finish *Blues in the Night* that way.

Why Was Improvisation So Common in Those Bygone Eras?

In previous centuries, sheet music was expensive, far more expensive than it is now, though it's still not too cheap today. It wasn't uncommon to see a music teacher with a limited supply of written music. To maximize the educational value of what they had, teachers taught students how to add to pieces and how to change them. Give this idea a try and see what happens. Play the piece as written and then play it again, embellishing the music as you see fit.

There are many ways to embellish melodies from baroque ornaments to blues licks. We can't go into those fancy things in this book because this book is primarily about music memory and music fun and not about improvisation. But a little understanding of improv methods can help you recognize it in the music you are playing and use it as a memory tool. Composers do it often to tweak their composition. They take a melody and create and develop it, change the ending, add extra notes, somehow elaborate the piece as it goes along. When you figure out the tricks, you have a heads-up on how the music is put together and that gives you an advantage in learning the piece.

Are You With Me?

If you are not sure what I mean, stop here and go on line and find a recording of Beethoven's *5th Symphony*. It starts off with one of the shortest and yet most recognizable melodies ever (the letter V of Morse Code dit dit dit dah). As you listen, note how the original melody comes back, changes, morphs, appears using different instruments, and is elaborated into a long and complex piece. Most of the classics are like this. They have a central musical idea that is then developed. Beethoven is a master of that kind of development. If you can recognize the central musical idea of your piece and its elaboration, you will be way ahead in your quest to put that piece in your repertoire. With all that in mind, let's see what the embellished sample might look like and let's play it on the piano:

Teacher White: That's my version of the melody. The original is there as before with an added part. I used the notes of the C major scale to embellish the melody. Now use your own ideas and find your own way to add to the original melody using the C major scale. It's not too painful. After you get the hang of it, it becomes fun.

Scale Recognition

Test your scale recognition on the following example from Bach. If you don't recognize the scale right away, what should you do?

Ex. 12

Answer: Analyze the music and THINK about it. If you get it great. No problem. If you don't get it. Great, no problem. It's even better if you don't get it because it means you may learn something. Remember the result is not as important as the brain effort to get to the result. Brain effort is what builds brain power. Look at measure two of this example. The half note is an A. Over the next three beats the notes go up the staff by step all the way to an A above the staff. Then there are three notes down to get to measure four.

Here are a couple of harder ones to try. The first one is from a famous Mozart sonata.

Notice on the second line there are three scales in a row for the right hand. If you can't see them, just look at the sixteenth notes.

Now the next example is hidden by the rhythm, so you would be best served by ignoring the rests between notes as you look at the Chopin mazurka.

Look at the first note in the right hand. It is an F, repeated. Then it goes to G, A, Bb, C, D, Eb, and so on all the way up to a high Bb with a trill on the end of it as if to announce that the scale is now over. How about that! The great Chopin in one of his most widely played mazurkas has for his melody, a simple scale.

Chromatic Scales

This scale uses a series of half steps from beginning to the end. Start on any note you wish and work up or down playing all the notes, black and white, in order. If you are unclear about the fingering, ask your teacher to show you. Chromatic scales are common and a gigantic chunking tool for learning a passage. Here is a great example of a chromatic scale from Chopin's *Fantasy Impromptu*. Chromatic scales are very easy to spot.

When we stop talking the talk and start walking the walk and actually begin memorizing *Fur Elise* by Beethoven, we'll have to play a chromatic passage starting well above middle C on a high A# and work down more than an octave. The fingering for that passage is straightforward, and knowing where to start and what fingering to use will allow you to get the entire passage down without much difficulty, and certainly without memorizing every note in the sequence. We will discuss the fingering of this chromatic passage when we reach the next volume. Meanwhile, let's finish up our discussion on scales with some thoughts on melody.

Melody Theory

Scales can be identified in music and recognized for what they are. They provide a great way to turn a long series of notes into an ordered single pattern that can be more easily memorized. However, scales are more than just stand-alone elements; they are the foundation from which melodic theory can be developed.

Yes, there is a theory of melody. If the word "theory" conjures up images of boring college lectures, relax. I am not writing a boring book—I'm trying to write an interesting book that is fun. So, let's have some fun with melody theory. But first, let's clarify what a theory is.

What is a Theory?

A theory is a group of ideas that helps organize (chunk, really) a rather large body of information and facts. Quantum mechanics, for example, is perhaps the best-confirmed scientific theory in history. It organizes facts about the behavior of atomic particles and allows scientists to use those facts to build atomic reactors or thermonuclear (hydrogen) bombs. Number theory explains much about numbers and why numbers in calculus work so well in explaining and predicting the movements of objects on Earth and in space. Similarly, music theory explains much of the organization and structure of music. Evolution explains most of the plant, animal, and human life on this planet. My Jesuit friend Father Meyers said, "If you don't believe in evolution, you are a fool. The only question is, did God have anything to do with it?"

Question: If music theory explains the organization and structure of music, what does melody theory explain?
Answer: Could it be the organization and structure of melody?

The Current State of Teaching Music Theory

Teacher Jimmy White often says, "The problem with music theory as it is taught in some places is that it is taught in a vacuum, completely separated from the music the student is actually studying. Consequently, students are seldom inspired to use this theory to create anything of interest. Besides, the theory taught in many American colleges these days is the theory of harmony [how chords are sequenced] and the theory of form [how a piece is organized into sections]. Little attention is paid to the part of a song that the audience will remember and be humming for the next three days—the melody."

Melody and Its Theory

A melody, usually born out of a scale, is that part of a song you can sing. In some songs, it has lyrics (words) added to it. We are using the major scale in the examples and exercises, but the same principles apply if you use any scale. All scales indicate what notes are in and what notes are out. So, major scales tell you what notes are in and what notes are out. The "in" notes are the notes you can use to create your melody. The "out" notes may not be used in the melody, but they can be used as fillers or for artistic purposes to add interest or complexity.

To start with, go to the piano and play a C major scale. We could use any major scale, but we start with the C major scale because it is the only major scale that uses only white notes. All other major scales use at least one black note. Once you understand the ideas using the C major scale, you can venture into other scales.

Play that C major scale, starting on middle C and moving up the piano using only white notes. Stop on the next highest C. Now play backward, back down until you return to middle C. If you cannot play a scale backward and forward easily, you are not ready to start making melodies using that scale. If you are having trouble playing this scale backward, play through it up and down until you can do it without any difficulty. Then come back to the book and read on.

Dichords and Trichords—Two Fundamental Flavors of Melody

Everything we are about to discuss will use the scale notes you just played in the C major scale. Always keep this in mind as you work through the exercises.

Two major building blocks for melodies exist: dichords and trichords.

Dichords

A dichord is simply two scale notes next to each other played one after the other. You can go up or down. Take two fingers on your right hand and play C-D. That is a dichord. Now play D-C. That is the same dichord in the opposite direction. Now pick a different note in the scale and play it, followed by the note one higher in the scale. Now reverse it and play the downward version. You can skip around and make a little melody yourself. If I were teaching you to improvise, I would go much further with this, but for the scope of this book, you get the idea.

Trichords

The trichord is similar to the dichord, but you must play three consecutive notes in the scale. Try playing C-D-E, then reverse directions and start on E. Now make an upward-moving trichord starting on G, and a downward-moving trichord starting on A. You can start on any note in the scale and go in either direction, up or down, playing three consecutive notes, and you are playing a trichord.

Since there are three notes in a trichord and only two notes in a dichord, the trichord has some melody shapes that dichords don't have. Trichords and dichords can both go straight up or down, but the trichord can do a twist, going up and then reversing and going down. Start on middle C and play C-E-D. That is a twisting trichord. It uses three consecutive notes in the C major scale, but just rearranges the order of the notes a bit. Now try D-E-C, and then E-C-D. As you can see, there are several ways to twist the trichord, but they are all considered twisting trichords. See how many different ways you can play a twisting trichord starting on the note F. Remember, you can only use the notes in the scale of C major because that is the scale we have chosen to play for this exercise. But, of course, in real life and real music, you could construct a trichord with the notes of any other scale.

Dichords and trichords make excellent chunking tools for your music memory. Currently, I am memorizing *Malagueña* from the Spanish Suite *Andalucia* by Ernesto Lecuona. It's in E major, and the melody is carried by the upper voice as ascending trichords with ascending or descending dichords. These trichords and dichords are nicely grouped into a rhythmic figure of two eighth notes followed by a quarter note (the trichord), then another two eighth notes followed by a quarter note (the next trichord), followed by two quarter notes (the dichord). As I know morse code, I remember the figure as UUM because U is ..and the next U is ..and the M is --, so the main rhythmic figure for the first part of the piece is dit dit dah dit dit dah dah dah (..-..--). The rhythmic figure is repeated ten times up to measure 21! Lecuona hung below these melody notes the lower notes of the major chords that have those melody notes as the fifth note of the chord. Why he did this I don't know, but I think it was to give the melody some density. Hence, we have C# major, which ends on G#, D major, which ends on A, and E major, which ends on B. But the melody is really carried by the upper note of these chords: G# A B G# A B A G#. Play this on your piano with the right rhythm and the right emphasis to see what I mean. Notice how this simple combination of trichords and dichords creates a famous melody. Notice that instead of a nebulous cloud of many notes to memorize, I am now, because of the analysis, better able to learn and understand the music. And get this: even if the analysis is considered wrong by some people, it still functions as a memory tool.

The Wannabe Trichord

Most great composers pick a scale within which to limit their melody. Doing so makes it much easier to play, easier to remember, easier to sing, and in general, much more enjoyable to the ear. There is another way, however, to play a trichord and use it to help make a melody, but it is controversial.

Play middle C followed by the E above it. This is what teacher Jimmy says is a trichord. I'm sure if I could see your face right now, you would either be giving me a puzzled look or smirking, thinking you just caught me in a mistake.

A smirk or a puzzled look? No, I am myself doing both. But I am going to keep an open mind and see what's up. Is it possible this trichord has only two notes?

I know, I know, I called it a trichord and then told you to play two notes. After all, a TRIchord is supposed to have three notes. This doesn't even meet the definition of a dichord because the two notes you just played are not next to each other in the scale.

Well, here's the controversial part. Jimmy's theory is that when we hear the note C followed by E, and we are oriented to the C major scale, our brain fills in the gap and actually hears the note D.

Controversial? Ho ho ho. When people hear things that aren't there, we physicians usually consider them psychotic and lock them up if they are a danger to themselves or others.

The further apart the two notes are, the harder it is for our brains to measure the distance between the notes. The brain cannot fill in the gap correctly when the gap between the notes gets too wide, so the brain resorts to guessing. Now, for very wide distances between notes, this guessing is acceptable, but not for the trichord. It is Jimmy's strong belief that most everyone can hear the gap between C and E, and their brain can fill in the one missing note.

Hear the gap, yes. Hear the missing note, no. Or at least I can't on my Essex, but on my Sauter, I sometimes think I can hear the D. My bet is that if we hooked people up to neurophysiological machines and measured their auditory evoked responses, we would find no auditory receptor activation for the unsounded pitch between the sounded C and E. If people do think they hear this middle unsounded note (D), it is probably a trick of the mind, a sonic illusion.

Teacher White: Yes, I can see this is controversial and is meeting with considerable resistance from those less in the know about music, like student Patten.

Student Patten: Exception! I resent this self-serving derogatory remark.

Teacher White: To continue, I call this a skipping trichord. You can begin on any note in your scale and go up or down, skipping the second note of the trichord and then playing the third note. Try a few, and you will hear the skipping, happy quality of these little gestures.

Student Patten: Yes, they are fun, and they do sound good. I have encountered them in great music by Debussy and more recently in the *Sonatina in G* by Beethoven. But why try to squeeze the skipping tones into a theory of melody based on trichords? Why not accept the idea that there is a third musical figure that can contribute to melody—what

Jimmy calls a skipping trichord and what I call an interval of a third? I am not sure, but I think if I worked on it, I could also construct a theory of melody based on perfect fourths and perfect fifths, or for that matter, on any other interval. Why not? To me, this skipping trichord is just a half chord. If it is a major third, it is the bottom of a major chord, and if it is a minor third, it is the top of a major chord. The chordal nature of the skipping trichord appears in Debussy, where he plants the trichords on the actual notes of a chord. Thus, Debussy might give us EGEGECECEC. Play this to see what I mean. Another example from *Music Box Dancer*: CGCECGC. This sounds better if you play the first G below the C and then play the second G above the C. My point is that from one view, some music looks like a collection of skipping trichords, and from another view, it looks like the C major chord played arpeggio. Which is it? Does it matter?

Teacher White: You may not completely agree with me that CE is actually a trichord, but in the music we will look at, we will see composer after composer using all three kinds of trichords (up/down, twisting, and skipping) to create their melodies.

Student Patten: I'm sure that's right, but so what? It doesn't prove your point.

Teacher White: Let's see how this looks in real music. In each of these examples, there are dichords and trichords. The first example comes from Schumann. When looking for dichords and trichords, the rhythm doesn't matter. In this case, there are rests between notes, but they are still phrased as if in pairs and threes.

This Faure piece has a beautiful melody. The song continues in the same fashion with great descending trichords and an occasional dichord thrown in.

Sometimes you will see slight deviations from the rule. This is what makes each composer unique. The great composers, either intuitively, or through years of music study, seem to know and easily interact with the foundational rules and forces of music. This is what unites their music and makes it satisfactory and fulfilling to the listener. The truly great ones, though, seem to have a knack for finding just the perfect place to break the rules or ignore the musical force. Some, in so doing, have discovered new rules and uncovered old forces, as of yet untapped, except by the most intuitive of composers.

Teacher White: I must include this next example. Even in what might be the most famous four notes in all of music, a skipping trichord is used:

We could spend all day analyzing famous songs, and we would consistently find the same patterns. Melodies are indeed made up of dichords and trichords. At the prestigious Juilliard School of Music in New York City, they also address tetrachords, pentachords, hexachords, and so on.

Teacher White: Those chords do exist, but I view them as I do the jazz scale. Jazz scales are fun, but you learn more by first studying and recognizing major scales. Only when major scales have been thoroughly mastered at all levels should you concern yourself with any of the other scale types. Similarly, with melody, you should focus on dichords and trichords until you have fully mastered them. Then, you can address something larger.

Student Patten: Enough is enough! Those who understand or want to use the dichord and trichord idea as a memory tool should do so. Those who don't understand it or wish to use a different system for memorizing patterns should do so as well.

Large Skips

What about bigger skips? When you see a large skip in the music that seems to be following a different rule of melody, it probably is. You could use the same rationale as with the skipping trichord and call these large skips some kind of skipping pentachord or octachord, right? Actually, I prefer to take a different approach. In my personal study, I have found a different pattern at work when you encounter something other than a dichord or a trichord. Recall our earlier discussion of chords, where we talked about how chords can be arpeggiated or blocked. Well, it's my belief that a melodic skip extending beyond the skipping trichord is usually jumping up or down to a note in the chord that's being played. The melody is actually helping fill out the chord.

It might seem odd for the melody to "help out the chord," but melody must align with the chords being played. In fact, there is a simple formula for how chords and melody work together: the melodic gesture must end on a chord tone. This is a great way to move a melody quickly from one register on the piano to another.

Melodic Gesture

Let me explain the formula I just mentioned: the melodic gesture must end on a chord tone. Instead of making a list like "the dichord, trichord, or skip to a chord tone must do this or that," I simply give one name to all of the melodic foundations that I've just addressed, and that name is "ta-da": the melodic gesture.

This fits because each little dichord or twisting trichord is a packet of emotion waiting to be unveiled. It is with each of these little devices that the pianist weaves their story as they play. "Chord tone" is simply a fancy name for the notes that make up a particular chord you are playing. So, when syncing up a melody to a chord, make sure that the melodic gesture ENDS on a note that is in the chord you are playing at that same moment. Don't worry about making the start of the melodic gesture match anything. If it sounds bad or clashing at first, your ear will quickly forgive you when you complete the melodic gesture with a tone that is in harmony with the chord. The end counts more than the beginning.

The Importance of Internal Dialogue

Wow! That was a lot about dichords and trichords, and I think most of it makes sense and will help with both understanding the nature of melody and memorizing music, especially if you talk to yourself about what's what. Internal dialogue and naming help the memory. Whether a trichord can skip a note or not doesn't seem to matter that much. I would just call the skip an incomplete trichord or a major third in the case of the distance from C to E. Having a name to organize and identify what you see on the music sheet is what helps memory. What you call that musical figure is of secondary importance. You could easily call the skipping trichord "Ralph" and the dichord "Fred." If Ralph and Fred help get the music into your memory—great! But actually, the names trichord and dichord serve better than Ralph and Fred because the names trichord and dichord remind us through embedded meaning of what the structure of the music actually is. Ralph doesn't tell us that three notes are involved, but trichord does. Of course, I could imagine other links that would remind me of what Ralph is and what Fred is. For instance,

I could tell myself Ralph and Fred are the small chords—either two or three notes. Because Ralph has more letters in his name than Fred, Ralph is the larger chord. Therefore, Ralph is the trichord and Fred is the dichord.

Do you see how this simple analysis of what a melody is doing could help you in memorizing a piece? It is all about chunking—taking the seemingly random set and seeing the patterns. And when there isn't a pattern or you don't see it, then imagine a pattern to help you memorize. Just as in chords, where you will find a certain composer tends to do a certain kind of arpeggio, you will also find certain composers tend to use predictable treatments in their melodic gestures. These patterns can be discovered and anticipated as you play a piece, and you can recall from one section to the next how similar or different the melodic pattern sequences are. Doing this will help as you memorize a piece. But it requires work and attention to details, noticing similarities and differences. It is like solving a puzzle, and it can be fun. Pareidolia is the perception of apparently significant patterns or recognizable forms or images, especially faces, in what is actually random or accidental arrangements. It's like cloud gazing. If the illusion of order helps with arrangement and memory, do it. But don't overdo it. Many people have seen Jesus in a burnt piece of toast or the Virgin Mary in a pile of rocks.

A few pages back, we were extolling the virtues of scales within a piece, and I have shown you how scales can help melodies. Now let's look at how scales determine the sequence of chords that are usually played. The intent is to combine what you have learned about chords with what you have learned about scales.

Chords and Scales

Recall that there are four different types of chords. Can you name them? If you can, great. If you can't, no problem—we will review them here. Review time is never wasted. Really solid learning often requires lots of review.

Review of Chord Types

If you start on middle C and make a major chord, then go up a half step to C# and make a major chord, and keep going up by a half step and making major chords, you will finally start repeating chords after 12 different major chords have been played. If you do the same thing with minor chords, there will also be 12 different minor chords before you start repeating.

If you look at augmented chords and start on C, you begin to repeat chords after playing only four different chords. The first chord, a C-augmented chord, is spelled C-E-G#. Go ahead and play the augmented chord starting on C#, then D, then Eb. Now play the augmented chord starting on E. It is spelled E-G#-C. It is the exact same notes as the C-augmented chord. Sure, it has a different name, but so do the black notes on the piano (F# and Gb). So, there are only four different augmented chords. Using the same logic, start making diminished chords beginning on the note C. How many different diminished chords are there? Stop, work it out, memorize the configuration and the notes involved, and then read on. Use four notes when working on these diminished chords.

You should have discovered that there are only three different diminished chords, each of which involves four different notes. If you got lost, here is how it works: The first chord would be spelled C-Eb-Gb-A (although the A might be called a B double flat—don't worry about it if this makes no sense to you). The diminished chord starting on C# would be quite different, as would the diminished chord starting on D. The chord starting on Eb would be spelled Eb-Gb-A-C. These are the same notes as the C-diminished chord. QED—Quod Erat Demonstrandum: When you use four notes, there are only three different diminished chords.

Here's the cool part. There are 12 major chords, 12 minor chords, four augmented chords, and three diminished chords. That's 31 total different chords—31 flavors of chords, just like there are 31 flavors of ice cream at Baskin Robbins. In reality, your music memory task is greatly simplified because instead of memorizing thousands of chords, you just need to have a working knowledge of 31.

Chord Placements

In a song or melody, chords are put into a series. Usually, a song or melody does not have just one chord for the entire song. The first chord is usually followed by a different chord. In fact, the song or melody typically changes chords several times, and maybe many, many times.

Chord Progression and Changes Are Not Random

This changing or sequencing of chords is called a chord progression. As a song progresses from the beginning to the end, the chord sequence progresses. Because the chord progression is not random, you can use the standard progressions as a memory tool. If the music follows the standard, you use the standard. If and when the music doesn't follow the standard, you use the standard as the memory tool and the departure from the standard as a memory tool. Compare and contrast! And keep thinking!

The language of music, even in lyrical modes, is a language of specific usage. It is about the arrangement, selection, presentation, organization, and control of sounds, as much as it is about what is sounded. The process of musical expression is, to me, scientific. Science is the process of investigation, observation, patterning through to hypothesis, testing and confirming, and rests on the scrutinizable and systematic acquisition of knowledge. When we use musical knowledge and understand the process of obtaining musical knowledge, then we do far less work than we might have had to do to get the same result we're after—mastery of performance.

Imagine a song with four chords in it. The first chord can be any one of 31 different chords. The second can also be one of 31 different chords. Already, you have 961 (31 x 31) possible combinations of chords. Choose from the same 31 chords for the third and fourth chords, and you now explode to an astronomical 923,521 (31 x 31 x 31 x 31) possible combinations—and that's with just four chords in the chord progression. Should you add just one more chord to the chord progression, you now have over 28 million combinations to sort through to find the ones that sound good together. Trust me, getting chords to sound good together is the goal of much of Western music, and it must be simpler than sorting through 28 million choices. Thank goodness it is!

Scales Limit, Organize, and Control Chord Progression

This is where scales come back into play. When we choose a scale, we commit ourselves to using only seven of the 12 possible tones on the piano. We call each of these seven tones "scale degrees." These seven scale degrees are the only notes allowed. Let's do a sample scale and then apply some basic deduction to figure out how scale affects the chords we can use in a song.

Play the C major scale on the piano. By using the C major scale, we limit ourselves to the white notes only.

Now for the deduction part: Starting on the note C, try making a major chord. Does it use all white notes, or does it contain a black note in the chord? Yes, it uses all white notes. It has to use white notes if it follows the major chord pattern. Now try a minor chord starting on C and see if it uses any black notes. It does use a black note, so we must throw that chord out. We cannot use that chord if we have selected the C major scale. Now try the augmented and diminished chords starting on C. Yet again, both of these chords use at least one black note, so we must throw them out. The only chord we can use that starts on C is the C major chord. We have just eliminated three chords that we know are no longer options. C is the first scale degree of our scale, so we will call this chord a "one chord" (a chord built on the first scale degree of the scale). If we are in C major, the only chord that can start on C is the C major chord. It must be major and only major.

We don't have to bother trying out any chords that start on C# because C# is not in our C major scale, so we will move on to the note D, the second note in our scale—the second scale degree. Let's try a D major chord. Oops, it has an F# in it. The D minor chord uses only white notes, so we can keep it. The D augmented chord uses two black notes, and the D diminished chord uses a G#. Once again, we are reduced to only one chord, a minor chord, that can be played in the C major scale. We will call this a "two chord." The two chord must be minor and only minor. In the case of the C major scale, the chord constructed on D is D minor. The two chord constructed on any major scale will always be minor.

Now you try it. Start on the third scale degree, the note E, and figure out which of the four kinds of chords you can play. Remember the criteria: You must use white notes and none other. If the chord uses even one black note, it is out.

If you played each of the four chord types correctly, you should have discovered that the only chord you can play starting on the note E is a minor chord. So, the third scale degree can only produce a minor chord. Call this the "three chord." The three chord constructed on any major scale is always minor.

Do you see a pattern? Each scale degree has one chord. The first scale degree is major, the second scale degree is minor, and the third scale degree is minor. Now you could go through all seven notes in the scale, reproduce this process, and discover that the fourth scale degree produces only a major chord, the fifth scale degree produces a major chord, and the 6th degree creates only a minor chord.

Quiz time: What chords are part of the C major scale if they start on the fourth, fifth, and sixth scale degree?

Answer: F major is fourth, G major is fifth, and A minor is sixth.

Go ahead and look at the seventh note of the scale. Start on B and see which chords you can make that only use the white notes. Count carefully, and then trust what you find. You might be wondering if you made a mistake, but you probably didn't. There are no three-note chords that you can make that use only white notes starting on B. There is no four-note diminished chord that you can make starting on B because the diminished chord would have to have a G#. If our math is correct, that means we have one chord, and only one chord, that we can make on each of the first six scale degrees, and that's it. We can't construct a chord on scale degree seven.

Isn't that nice? We just reduced our choices of chords in any one scale down to six!

Using the probability calculus from earlier, with five chords in a chord progression, we have gone from 28 million choices down to 7,776 (6 x 6 x 6 x 6 x 6). That still seems like a lot of choices, but in one page of this book, we have just eliminated 27,992,224 choices. Here's the best part: these six chords actually go together in predictable patterns, so it's actually far, far fewer choices than 8,000. The usual patterns are to start at the one chord, play it, then play many different chords in the key, and end up on the five chord followed by a return to one.

As you can see, music becomes much more manageable when you combine knowledge of chords with an understanding of how scales work. This melding of these two concepts is at least 500 years old. What I've just been describing is the internal workings of a "key." Many of you have played music in different keys. You have been taught to read the "key signature" and remember to play those sharps or flats throughout the piece, whether or not the sharps or flats are written in the body of the music. You might have been taught the cadence and scale for that particular key, but now you understand something of what is behind this information and how and why it works.

The Nature of Key

A scale is what determines the notes that are in and the notes that are out in a particular "key." This scale determines what melodic gestures can be used in the song, and it shows you what chords are in and what chords are out. The "key" tells you what the home note is and what the home chord is going to be. Trust me when I tell you that the music you are studying right now was written by someone who understood these facts inside and out. The music of the great composers is stuffed full of these elements. But with each new piece, you must discover the relationships for yourself and then use your knowledge of these relationships to facilitate your memory.

Now that we have established the idea of chords in a key, there are many different directions we could go. If you were learning to improvise, I would delve into chord tendencies and show you some of the universal patterns of chord progressions. For the scope of this book, I needn't do that. Let's just use these facts about chords in the key to notice repeated patterns in an individual song. Let me show you a short passage of music and let you see the chord progression it contains. Later on, you will use this skill to see the chord progression in *Fur Elise*.

What's it all about? Why does the bass start in A minor and end in a form of E?

Over time, as you play several pieces by the same composer, you'll start to notice patterns in how they use chords, chord patterns, melodic gestures, and chord progressions. This is why Debussy sounds like Debussy and not like Chopin. When you begin to analyze these elements, you'll uncover a whole new world of connections. You'll see beyond the music on the page to the composer sitting in a room somewhere, crafting the piece you are now trying to master.

The Secrets of Music Are Analogous to the Secrets of Literature

Music and literature are different systems of knowledge. Literature can include linguistically innovative ideas as well as straightforward declarations. Parataxis, conventional end-stopped lines and enjambment, narrative description, metaphor and metonymy, indirect discourse, and other language tools are all part of a process in literature aimed at confronting hierarchies and imposed structures related to life—usually human life itself. Literature is art, and art imitates life, whereas actual living is primarily action and emotion.

Chords and scales, harmony and melody, and other musical tools are all part of a process in music aimed at something even more abstract than literature, yet deeply human and deeply felt. The writer works from the inside to open a view of the outside and the whole of the human experience through language. The average reader doesn't know or care about the art and science of effective writing; they're just reading and enjoying the story.

Similarly, the musician works from the inside to open a view of the whole. The average audience doesn't know or care about the art and science of effective music composition and performance; they're just listening and enjoying the music.

The Secrets of Music Are Analogous to the Wizard of Oz

All of this might remind you of the scene in *The Wizard of Oz* where Dorothy and her friends are in the chamber of the Great Oz. They are in awe of the power and mystery of what they see. Just as the group is nearly overwhelmed by the moment, Toto, Dorothy's dog, pulls on a cord and exposes the little old man behind the curtain.

Music can be like the Great Oz. With the tools to deeply explore and analyze the great music set before you, you can pull back the curtain and see the ordinary tools used by the men and women who are manipulating the levers connected to the great moving force we call music.

The End of Part II

This is the end of Part II. But before we move on to the next volume and the practical applications of our memory training, I want to show you what ChatGPT has to say about the piano. I asked for a 1,000-word essay praising the piano, and in a matter of seconds, I got the following. Look it over. It makes sense, and I detect no errors in diction, grammar, syntax, spelling, and so forth. But to me, it seems dry, lifeless, and boring. I could tell it was produced by a machine. I learned in creative writing class that the hallmark of all amateur writing is the lack of conflict on every page. If that's true, the ChatGPT essay looks like the work of an amateur. See what you think.

Note: Although I asked for 1,000 words, I got 1,206, suggesting some tendency of the program toward logorrhea.

The Elegance and Grandeur of the Piano: A Celebratory Ode

Throughout the annals of music history, there exists an instrument that stands as an emblem of timeless elegance and grandeur, an instrument that has woven itself into the very fabric of human culture and artistry. This exquisite creation, the piano, possesses a transcendent charm and musical versatility that has captivated the hearts and minds of countless individuals across the globe. With its rich history, evocative sound, and unparalleled contribution to the world of music, the piano is an instrument deserving of resounding praise and admiration.

The piano's journey through time is a testament to its enduring appeal. Its origins can be traced back to the early 18th century, when Bartolomeo Cristofori, an Italian instrument maker, invented the first pianoforte. This groundbreaking innovation marked a significant departure from its predecessor, the harpsichord, as it allowed musicians to vary the intensity of sound by controlling the force with which the keys were struck. This invention revolutionized music composition and performance, forever changing the musical landscape.

The piano's evolution is a story of continuous improvement and innovation. Over the centuries, it has seen numerous modifications, culminating in the modern grand and upright pianos we see today. The virtuoso craftsmanship behind each instrument is a testament to human ingenuity and dedication. Meticulous attention to detail, from the exquisite woodwork to the precision engineering of the keys and strings, results in instruments that are not only melodically enchanting but also visually stunning.

One of the piano's most compelling qualities is its remarkable versatility. It can bridge the gap between genres and eras, seamlessly traversing the diverse landscapes of classical, jazz, pop, rock, and many more. It can evoke a wide range of emotions, from the soothing, introspective melodies of Debussy's *Clair de Lune* to the electrifying, rhythmic patterns of Gershwin's *Rhapsody in Blue.* This ability to adapt and mold itself to the artist's intentions has earned the piano its revered status in the world of music.

The piano's vast dynamic range is a source of endless fascination and inspiration. Its ability to whisper gently or thunder dramatically, from the softest pianissimo to the most thunderous fortissimo, allows musicians to convey the most nuanced emotions. A well-played piano piece can transport listeners through a journey of feelings, transcending language barriers and cultural boundaries. It has been the medium through which countless composers and musicians have channeled their innermost thoughts and sentiments, leaving a timeless legacy of sound that continues to resonate with audiences worldwide.

Moreover, the piano's role in shaping the classical music tradition cannot be overstated. It has been at the forefront of some of the most iconic compositions in history, from the delicate sonatas of Mozart and Beethoven to the passionate nocturnes of Chopin. Its adaptability and expressive capabilities have made it the quintessential instrument for many renowned composers. Beethoven, in particular, revolutionized piano composition with his sonatas, pushing the boundaries of what could be achieved on this magnificent instrument. His *Moonlight Sonata*, a piece that explores the depths of human emotion, remains a perennial favorite and a testament to the piano's enduring impact on classical music.

In the realm of jazz, the piano has carved out a unique niche for itself. With its expressive potential and harmonic richness, it has been a canvas for improvisation and innovation. Legends like Duke Ellington, Thelonious Monk, and Bill Evans have graced the keys of the piano with their genius, ushering in a new era of musical exploration. Jazz piano, characterized by its intricate harmonies and syncopated rhythms, continues to inspire and captivate audiences to this day.

The piano's influence extends to the world of popular music as well. It has been a driving force behind many iconic songs, from the mesmerizing ballads of Elton John to the electrifying rock anthems of Queen. In the hands of rock legends like Jerry Lee Lewis and Billy Joel, the piano has taken on a rebellious, exuberant spirit, commanding attention with its percussive energy and melodic prowess. Its ability to seamlessly integrate with various instruments and genres is a testament to its adaptability and universality.

PIANO BY HEART

The piano also holds a special place in the hearts of those who appreciate its solo beauty. The image of a solitary pianist, immersed in the music, is an evocative and timeless one. Playing the piano requires a profound connection between the musician and the instrument, demanding technical skill and emotional depth. The process of practicing and mastering this instrument is a journey of self-discovery, discipline, and personal growth.

In addition to its role in classical, jazz, and popular music, the piano has been a vital educational tool. It is often the first instrument that aspiring musicians encounter in their musical journey. Learning to play the piano imparts a solid foundation in music theory and ear training, and it equips students with essential skills that can be applied to other instruments as well. The piano's layout, with its distinct keys and clear visual representation of notes, makes it accessible to beginners, while also providing endless opportunities for advanced musicians to explore complex compositions.

The piano's cultural significance extends beyond its musical contributions. It has appeared in countless works of art and literature, symbolizing everything from romanticism to nostalgia. Its image has been imprinted in our collective consciousness, gracing the pages of novels, poetry, and paintings. The piano's ability to stir emotions and evoke vivid memories is a testament to its enduring cultural relevance.

In addition to its artistic and cultural influence, the piano has played a vital role in social and communal life. It has been a centerpiece in homes, salons, and concert halls, bringing people together to celebrate the joy of music. Gathered around the piano, families have created cherished memories, and friends have shared moments of musical bliss. The piano has been the heart of countless gatherings, uniting people through the power of its melodies.

The piano's enduring legacy also includes its influence on technology and innovation. The development of the piano led to advancements in acoustics, mechanics, and engineering. The piano's evolution from acoustic instruments to digital keyboards has expanded its accessibility and versatility even further. It has become an integral part of contemporary music production and recording, offering musicians a wide range of sounds and effects.

In conclusion, the piano is a remarkable instrument that deserves wholehearted praise and admiration. Its rich history, versatility, and influence on music, culture, and society make it an enduring symbol of elegance and grandeur. The piano has touched the hearts of countless individuals, from the most renowned composers and virtuosos to beginners taking their first steps in music. Its ability to convey emotions, from the deepest melancholy to the highest exuberance, is a testament to its timeless allure.

The piano's continued relevance in our modern world is a testament to its enduring appeal. As we celebrate the piano, we not only honor the instrument itself but also pay homage to the countless musicians, composers, and enthusiasts who have contributed to its legacy. In an age of ever-changing trends and technologies, the piano stands as a steadfast and timeless reminder of the power of music to unite, inspire, and elevate the human spirit.

www.ingramcontent.com/pod-product-compliance
Lightning Source LLC
LaVergne TN
LVHW021815060526
838201LV00058B/3388